THE FUTURE OF ROMAN
CATHOLIC THEOLOGY

THE
FUTURE
OF
ROMAN
CATHOLIC
THEOLOGY

Vatican II—Catalyst for Change

George A. Lindbeck

FORTRESS PRESS
PHILADELPHIA

To

Vi, fellow observer, and
Kris, who gained many Fathers
and Mothers in Christ in Rome

CONTENTS

FOREWORD

Like a star shell lighting up no-man's-land, this brilliant analysis of the theology of Vatican II illuminates the contours of a new and often confusing frontier. In a remarkable *tour de force* Professor Lindbeck dares to deal in a brief compass not just with selected documents but with the entire corpus produced by the Council, as he singles out motifs and directions. It is this that distinguishes his holistic, systematic analysis of basic trends from numerous other reports.

For Professor Lindbeck, Vatican II is not merely a compromise between a more static past and a more volatile present. He sees its dynamic factors as those that will shape the future. He is less interested in where the Roman Catholic Church is at the moment than in where it is going, as attested by the moving, fluid elements in its theology and practice.

Organized around the theme of the church in mission, Lindbeck's analysis begins with a breathtaking panorama of the fresh eschatological view that shapes the newer theology of the Council. The nature of the world and of man is not seen primarily under the sign of a biblical realism that dwells only on contemporary depravity and sin. Instead, the present with all its crises is seen from the vantage point of the future. As Wolfhart Pannenberg has pointed out, in the biblical *Weltanschauung* the nature of things is determined out of the future. What they are is determined by what becomes of them. Therefore, creation happens from the end even more than from the beginning. Because Lindbeck ardently shares such an eschatological faith, his view, while eschewing all easy optimism, is necessarily hope-filled.

Amid the more sober realities of this post-conciliar period, some may be moved to criticize Lindbeck as exhibiting an unrealistic irenicism. Certainly, he cannot be classified among those whose actions seem to parody Martin Luther's explanation of the Eighth Commandment, "Thou shalt not bear false witness," to read, with regard to the neighbor: "Attack him, speak ill of him, and put the worst construction on everything."

Others may accuse him of being a minimalist who is "too soon made glad," too easily satisfied with the encouraging biblical and evangelical trends within the Roman communion. However, has not the church in all its branches and throughout its long history suffered many things at the hands of earnest, well-meaning maximalists? Not content with the naked Scriptures, they put protective hedges about the Word like the ancient scribes. And soon various schools are shooting at each other from their various outer breastworks, each one persuaded that if their puny man-made bulwark is overrun, the divine citadel of the faith will fall. But when men seek to protect the seeming defenselessness of the faith with their petty human securities, instead of allowing the almighty Word to defend itself, they are actually forsaking the faith and making flesh their arm.

Lindbeck rejoices over the very real changes that have come about in the Roman Church's view of itself and its mission. He suggests some ingenious possibilities for reconciling certain massive outstanding differences. Throughout, however, he stands firm on the essentials of his scriptural Lutheran faith. For example, precisely because he is no maximalist in his view of the Scriptures, refusing to make of them a paper papacy, he clears the way for Roman Catholics to be minimalists in their view of the prerogatives of the bishop of Rome.

Lindbeck holds a functional understanding of the church. He speaks of it primarily in terms of witness, service, and worship. This dynamic ecclesiology lends itself particularly well to the concept of the church in mission.

Lindbeck would feel very much at home with the definition of mission advanced by one of its outstanding conservative Lutheran proponents, Wilhelm Loehe, who a century ago described mission as "the one church of God in motion."

The author's exposition of the mission of God exercised through a church divided yet pressing for reconciliation will be read with keen interest by a large number of lay people and scholars in all Christian communions and beyond. No one who wishes to speak authoritatively on Protestant–Roman Catholic relations, on Vatican II, or on the mission of God through his whole church can afford to ignore this keen analysis.

WILLIAM J. DANKER
Editor, Church-in-Mission Series

PREFACE

This book originated in lectures given at the Institute on the Church in Mission held at Concordia Lutheran Theological Seminary, St. Louis, Missouri, in August, 1966. Never have I met more intense theological interest in a similar gathering. I was both stimulated and encouraged, and for this I would like to thank the "separated Lutheran brethren" from the Missouri Synod who invited, listened to, and discussed these lectures with me.

My debt is even greater to the Vatican Secretariat for Christian Unity and to the many bishops and theological experts who assembled for the Second Vatican Council. Their Christian warmth and openness towards us who were observers made us participants, not simply spectators. Because of them, my interpretation of the theology of the Council has benefited far more than could be indicated in the following pages from personal notes and memories.

Nor can I leave unmentioned the contributions of the leaders of the Lutheran World Federation, who sent me as a delegated observer to Rome, and of the officers of Yale University, who released me for a two-year period from my academic duties so that I could go. Without their trust and confidence, this book would not have been written.

Yet the help which I cherish most has come from my wife and daughter. They were with me for the two years in Rome entertaining bishops, priests, monks, nuns and even laymen and women, thereby opening up a world of human relations at the heart of the council which would have remained closed to me if I had led a bachelor's life. Kris did her share as only a two-to-four-year old can, while Vi, in addition to the cooking and cleaning inseparable from entertaining, supplied some of the keenest theological insights I gained from anyone, whether Protestant observer or Catholic participant.

ABBREVIATIONS

The titles of the documents of Vatican II are consistently given in their English form in the text of this book. Abbreviations are also based on the translations rather than the official Latin titles. For the convenience of the scholar, the list below indicates the English abbreviation, followed by the conventional Latin abbreviation in parentheses, and the full English and Latin titles. Numbers which follow most of the abbreviations in the text refer to the articles into which the conciliar documents are divided. Thus, *SL 4* refers to the Constitution on the Sacred Liturgy, article 4.

AL   (AL)   Decree on the Apostolate of the Laity *(Decretum de apostolatu laicorum)*

BPO   (EM)   Decree on the Bishops' Pastoral Office in the Church *(Decretum de pastorali episcoparum munere)*

C   (LG)   Dogmatic Constitution on the Church *(Lumen gentium. Constitutio dogmatica de ecclesia)*

CE   (EC)   Declaration on Christian Education *(Declaratio de educatione christiana)*

CMA   (AG)   Decree on the Church's Missionary Activity *(Ad gentes. Decretum de activitate missionali ecclesiae)*

CMW   (GS)   Pastoral Constitution on the Church in the Modern World *(Gaudium et spes. Constitutio pastoralis de ecclesia in mundo huius temporis)*

DR   (DV)   Dogmatic Constitution on Divine Revelation *(Dei verbum. Constitutio dogmatica de divina revelatione)*

E   (UR)   Decree on Ecumenism *(Unitatis redintegratio. Decretum de oecumenismo)*

EC   (OE)   Decree on Eastern Catholic Churches *(Orientalium ecclesiarum. Decretum de ecclesiis orientalibus catholicis)*

IC   (IC)   Decree on the Instruments of Social Communication *(Decretum de instrumentis communicationis)*

ABBREVIATIONS

MLP (PM) Decree on the Ministry and Life of Priests *(Decretum de presbyterorum ministerio et vita)*

NCR (RN) Declaration on the Relationship of the Church to Non-Christian Religions *(Declaratio de ecclesiae habitudine ad religiones non-christianas)*

PF (IS) Decree on Priestly Formation *(Decretum institutione sacerdotali)*

RF (DH) Declaration on Religious Freedom *(Dignitatis humanae. Declaratio de libertate religiosa)*

RL (PC) Decree on the Appropriate Renewal of Religious Life *(Perfectae caritatis. Decretum accommodata renovatione vitae religiosae)*

SL (SL) Constitution on the Sacred Liturgy *(Constitutio de sacra liturgia)*

DS H. Denzinger and A. Schönmetzer, *Enchiridion Symbolorum* (32d ed.; Freiburg: Herder & Co., 1963)

INTRODUCTION

I

What is new in the theology of the Second Vatican Council? What effect will this have on the thinking of the Roman Catholic Church? What will be the results for the historic controversies between Catholics and Protestants?

The chapters which follow outline one set of answers to these questions; but before launching into exposition, it will be useful to indicate the general character of these answers and the considerations which have led to their formulation.

I believe that the conciliar documents reflect a genuinely new vision of the world. This vision supplies an all-encompassing framework within which Roman Catholic views of the church and its mission are undergoing notable transformations. The first chapter sketches this new framework, while the second and third chapters show how it is related to profound reinterpretations of the basic nature, "secular" mission, and worship of the church. In these areas, the old issues between Roman Catholicism and the Reformation are being dissolved or radically recast. When looked at from the new perspectives, positions which have been traditionally opposed now appear to be complementary aspects of a fuller grasp of Christian truth. There are also areas in which Roman Catholic dogmas, even when radically reinterpreted, still affirm what the Reformation is committed to denying. These disagreements diminish the possibilities of *rapprochement* sketched in the first three chapters. I shall argue, however, in chapters four and five, that the new approaches authorized by Vatican II are nevertheless making possible a Roman Catholic view of the structure of the church and its dogmatic authority which is perhaps not incompatible with the Reformation.

What differentiates this study of the Council from most other interpretations is that it attempts to penetrate beneath the multiplicity of themes and formulations to identify the unique features of the theology of Vatican II. This is a risky enterprise, and has so far been little attempted for the Council as a whole (though a great many of the essays dealing with particular documents or doctrines have been of this type). I know of only one comparable effort, a brief article entitled "Balance Sheet of the Council"[1] by the Dutch Dominican, Father E. Schillebeeckx. In it he has well described the nature of the endeavor:

The council documents can be examined with an eye for the leading thought which consciously or unconsciously guided the entire council theme. This can produce varying results and a certain subjective interpretation cannot be ruled out. Nevertheless the concrete contents of all the documents can be allowed so to affect one that on the ground of these contents one suddenly finds a single basic thought which is illuminated from different angles in the various documents. This is not to say that the Council itself has consciously and thematically seen, grasped and developed this basic thought. As in the life of humans, so in the life of the Church also there are initially more or less unconscious basic intuitions which guide the entire seeking and thinking; it is only in the result that this basic intuition can be thematised or made consciously reflexive.

"This," he adds, "is what I want to try and do." It is also what we shall attempt. My analyses of the basic themes of the Council are not at all the same as those of Father Schillebeeckx, but they are not, I think, incompatible.

In an effort of this kind, the dangers of what Schillebeeckx calls "subjective interpretation" are so great that some explanation is in order. My own reason for adopting this approach is that I know of no other way of formulating even a tentative opinion on how the Council documents should be understood. In themselves,

[1] E. Schillebeeckx, "Balance Sheet of the Council," "Information Documentation on the Conciliar Church" (mimeographed; via S. Maria Dell' Anima, 30, Rome, 1966), Dossier 66–1, p. 2.

they are often ambiguous, open to both rigidly "conservative" and radically "progressive" exegesis. The decision on the proper way to read them depends on how one evaluates their general tenor, on how one views their place and probable influence on the vast changes in theological thinking now taking place in the Roman Catholic Church as well as in other churches.

This is obvious when one considers that Vatican II represents a transitional phase in a movement which began long before it was convoked and will continue to develop far into the future. It embodies (and thereby approves and stimulates) fresh currents of thought. However, like all transitional events it is an amalgam of the new and the old. Its documents are often compromises between stale and tired ways of thinking and fresh and vital ones. Sometimes they are even deliberately ambiguous;[2] the only way to rally a consensus from bishops of all parties was to clothe the new in old language (or the old in new language) so that what was said would at least be tolerable, even if not satisfying, to both conservatives and progressives. As a result, the texts often fall short of the best in contemporary Roman Catholic theology; they fall short, in some cases, of what even those primarily responsible for the drafting would have liked to say.

This indicates the necessity of not simply taking them as they stand. Merely repeating or summarizing them, however accurately, can give a positively misleading impression of the present and future course of Roman Catholic thought.

It seems to me that this mistake is made by many skeptical commentators who strive to be "soberly realistic" about the extent of the present Catholic renewal. They interpret the Council legalistically and non-situationally in a kind of hermeneutical vacuum, sealed off from consideration of the concrete situation in which it took place. In order to avoid overoptimism, they refuse to be impressed by any except the most unequivocal changes. They resolve all ambiguities in favor of interpretations which are most

---

[2] For a discussion of some of the ambiguities in one document, see G. Lindbeck, "The Church: A Protestant Point of View," *Vatican II: An Interfaith Appraisal,* ed. J. H. Miller (Notre Dame, Ind.: University of Notre Dame Press, 1966), pp. 219–30.

in continuity with rigid versions of Tridentine and Vatican I conservatism.

My own view, in contrast, is that because the Council is part of a dynamic, ongoing process, it is the *new* theological emphases which are likely to prove most significant as a basis and guide for further developments. As a matter of fact, the majority of the most active drafters and interpreters of the documents understand them as favoring fresh approaches.

The correctness of this hermeneutical procedure is confirmed when one considers past councils and doctrinal pronouncements. Their import has been determined by what is new in them, by the redirection they have given the thinking of the church. The Council of Trent, for example, was in some respects less rigid, defensive, and anti-Protestant than the post-Tridentine Catholicism it helped to mold. But the fundamentally new fact about that council was that in it the Reformation had been dogmatically rejected, and this both reflected and furthered a process in which the repudiation of the Reformers' views on justification, faith, grace, and the relation of Scripture and tradition became far more total and massive than it was at Trent itself.[3] Something like this seems likely to happen as a result of Vatican II—though now, we may hope, in the reverse direction.

There can be no absolute guarantee that the new direction will be pursued, but we are most likely to be correct about the long-range theological significance of the recent council if we concentrate on what is new in it. We must concentrate on describing and understanding the patterns of thought which make Vatican II theologically distinctive and radically different from the two previous councils and the last four hundred years of Roman Catholic dogmatic development. While not overlooking the old, we should remember that it will probably be of diminishing im-

---

[3] Newer and older Catholic interpretations of the Tridentine teachings on justification, faith, and grace are briefly compared by W. Joest, "The Doctrine of Justification of the Council of Trent," *Lutheran World*, IX (1962), 204–18. In reference to Scripture and tradition, the change in the interpretation of Trent is described by the scholar who has done most to bring it about: J. R. Geiselmann, "Scripture, Tradition, and the Church: An Ecumenical Problem," in *Christianity Divided*, ed. D. J. Callahan *et al.* (New York: Sheed & Ward, 1961), pp. 39–72.

portance. It is convictions such as these which provide the basis for the following attempt to describe the new understanding of world, church, and mission which began to emerge at Vatican II.

II

The major themes of this book correspond to those of the Council. I have dealt with "world" in chapter one and with "church and mission" in the following four chapters. "Church and mission" is handled as a single topic because, according to one strong strain of thought at the Council, "church *is* mission." This means that its essence is to be a sacramental sign or witness to God's saving work in all that it is and does. It exercises this witnessing or missionary function in its *diakonia* or secular service of the world (chapter two), its *leitourgia* or worship of God (chapter three), and its *koinonia* or communal unity expressed both interpersonally and in institutional structures (chapter four) and in common faith and dogma (chapter five).

This pattern of exposition reflects the inner logic, though not always the external divisions, of the Council's sixteen documents. Their task, according to Pope John XXIII, is that of "updating" the church in both its structures and teaching so that it will be able to carry out its mission in the world more effectively.[4] Thus the Constitution on the Church is by general agreement the centerpiece of the Council. It is complemented by the Constitution on the Church in the Modern World. This is much the longest of the documents, containing nearly one-fourth of the one hundred thousand words which the Council produced. Most of it is devoted to an analysis and evaluation of the contemporary world.

---

[4] "We . . . have felt immediately the urgency of the duty to call our sons together, to give the Church the possibility to contribute more efficaciously to the solution of the problems of the modern world." *The Documents of Vatican II,* ed. Walter M. Abbott (New York: Herder & Herder and Association Press, 1966), p. 705. In the opening speech of the Council, John XXIII spoke of his hope that "by bringing herself up to date [*aggiornamento*] where required . . . the Church will make men, families, and peoples really turn their minds to heavenly things" (*ibid.,* p. 712). It should be noted that normally the translations of the Council documents contained in this Abbott edition will be cited, although there will be occasional changes in the wording where, in the judgment of the author, this improves the translation.

Other aspects of the external relations of the church are dealt with by the Decrees on the Church's Missionary Activity and on Ecumenism and the Declarations on the Relationship of the Church to Non-Christian Religions and on Religious Freedom. Two major documents, the Constitutions on Divine Revelation and on the Sacred Liturgy, are not formally concerned with the church and its mission, but they are nevertheless of great importance for both themes when these are broadly conceived. All the other conciliar actions are attempts to implement in specific areas the understanding of the church and its mission enunciated in the theologically basic documents. This is true of the Declaration on Christian Education and the Decrees on the Instruments of Social Communication, Eastern Catholic Churches, the Bishops' Pastoral Office in the Church, Priestly Formation, the Appropriate Renewal of the Religious Life, the Apostolate of the Laity, and the Ministry and Life of Priests. In short, there is no better rubric than "World, Church, and Mission" under which to present a comprehensive sketch of the main features of the theology of the Council.

Not all the documents of the Council are of equal importance for our purposes. There will be few references to the last eight named above. Several of these, most notoriously the Decree on Communications, are of such poor quality that they seem unlikely to exert much influence.

A brief commentary such as the present one cannot engage in a detailed examination of the texts it discusses, nor provide background information regarding their history. It presupposes some knowledge of the Council and its work such as is supplied by many books now on the market.[5]

[5] The Abbott edition of *The Documents of Vatican II* (see n. 4, above) is the most helpful single book available to English-speaking readers, not only because it contains all the documents in an acceptable translation, but also because it includes helpful introductions and commentaries by both Catholics and non-Catholics. For scholarly work, the best single tool is the three-volume supplement to the *Lexikon für Theologie und Kirche. Das Zweite Vatikanische Konzil. Dokumente und Kommentare* (Freiburg: Herder & Co., 1966–68).

The most extensive non-Catholic commentary on the Council is provided by a series of three books spanning the period from before the Council to its conclusion: *The Papal Council and the Gospel*, ed. K. E. Skydsgaard (Minneapolis: Augsburg Publishing House, 1961); *Dialogue on the Way*, ed. G. A. Lindbeck (Minneapolis: Augsburg Publishing House, 1965); and *Challenge and Response*,

One background question is so frequently raised, however, that it must be mentioned here. Protestants often ask about the authority of the conciliar pronouncements. This is a complex problem.[6] Vatican II, in contrast to all previous councils, deliberately viewed its task as pastoral. It refrained from formally specifying any of its teachings as dogmas in the full sense (as *de fide*) and directed no anathemas against those who might reject them. Nevertheless, some of its formulations are presented in such a way that they seem likely to have the practical force of dogmas, at least in the sense that no responsible Catholic theologian or spokesman will publicly deny them or suggest that his church might later reverse them. The decisions in favor of religious liberty, of the sacramentality and collegiality of the episcopacy, and of the "general priesthood" of all believers are examples of pronouncements bearing such authority.

This does not mean that other teachings are not also binding in various degrees. In general, the "constitutions," especially the dogmatic constitutions, are supposed to have the highest authority. "Declarations" and "decrees" stand on a lower level (although one of the examples of quasi-dogmatic teaching which I have mentioned, that on religious freedom, is contained in a declaration). For our purposes, it is enough to say that the doctrines of the Council, while in most cases presented as pastoral directives and as guidance for the church, are nevertheless of such force that

ed. W. A. Quanbeck and V. Vajta (Minneapolis: Augsburg Publishing House, 1966). For interesting Protestant accounts see Robert M. Brown, *Observer in Rome* (New York: Doubleday & Co., 1964); and Albert C. Outler, *Methodist Observer at Vatican II* (Westminster, Md.: Newman Press, 1967). A provocatively tendentious view is provided by Paul Blanshard, *Paul Blanshard on Vatican II* (Boston: Beacon Press, 1966).

The most extensive Catholic account in English is the four-volume series by X. Rynne, *Letters from Vatican City* (1963), *The Second Session* (1964), *The Third Session* (1965), and *The Fourth Session* (1966) (New York: Farrar, Straus & Giroux, 1963–66). A highly readable journalistic treatment of the first session is R. B. Kaiser's *Pope, Council and World: The Story of Vatican II* (New York: Macmillan Co., 1963); and of the second, Michael Novak, *The Open Church: Vatican II, Act II* (New York: Macmillan Co., 1964). The entire Council is reported on in a helpful but very personal way by R. E. Tracy, *American Bishop at the Vatican Council* (New York: McGraw-Hill Book Co., 1966).

See also *Vatican II: An Interfaith Appraisal* (see n. 2, above).

[6] J. Neumann, "Die Verbindlichkeit der Beschlüsse," *Die Autorität der Freiheit. Gegenwart des Konzils und Zukunft der Kirche im ökumenischen Disput*, ed. J. C. Hampe (Munich: Kösel-Verlag, 1967), I, 77–85.

the official organs and agents of the church, and individual Catholics as well, are obligated to follow them as quickly and fully as feasible.

Any body of teaching, including that presented by the Council, is open to diverse interpretations. Its actual impact on those who seek to be faithful to it depends on what they bring to it, that is, the framework and situation in terms of which they understand it. This is what makes it possible for both conservatives and progressives to accommodate themselves to the Council. Yet in the long run the most common framework of interpretation is likely to be the one related to the new theological emphases in the documents. The old will be understood in terms of the new, rather than vice versa. This, at least, is the perspective within which the following analysis proceeds.

1

VISION OF A
WORLD RENEWED

To explain what Vatican II says about the church and its functions, we must first describe the new theological vision of the world which influenced its pronouncements. This new vision of the world supplies an all-encompassing framework within which the theology of the past is now being interpreted. In the course of this reinterpretation the older theology is undergoing notable changes.

This vision is only fragmentarily reflected in the conciliar documents. In order fully to recognize its presence we must first recall how it is being articulated by those thinkers who created the theological milieu in which the Council's work was done and is being interpreted. Only at the end of this chapter will we turn to a consideration of the conciliar texts themselves.

This new vision grows out of a new understanding of biblical eschatology together with the acceptance of the secular-scientific world view. The latter is familiar enough in its general outline. The former, the biblical eschatology, should be explained. It is an eschatology that is neither wholly "realized," as in much contemporary theological existentialism, nor "otherworldly," as traditional eschatology is nowadays generally said to have been. We could label it "realistically futuristic" eschatology. The kingdom of God on earth, according to this view, is not actualized exclusively and completely in Christ's first coming or in the event of faith; rather, its full manifestation is really and temporally future. Further, the kingdom is conceived of as the transformation of the real world. It is not simply "beyond," as in customary ways of imagining heaven; nor is the realm of space, time, and history in which we live pictured as moving towards total destruction at the end of time, but rather as in the process of being prepared to become the kingdom of our God. This is a theological interpretation of the modern, secular picture of the world in terms of a biblical outlook which has been largely lost sight of through most of Christian history.

This vision of the world has its roots in theological developments of the last century and a half, ranging from the emergence of historical awareness in F. C. Baur, J. A. Moehler, and John Henry Newman to the eschatological emphases in contemporary figures as diverse as Karl Barth and Rudolf Bultmann. Only in the period since the Second World War does it acquire the particular features which we have just mentioned. Teilhard de Chardin is doubtless the most famous representative of a realistically futuristic eschatological interpretation of the modern world view,[1] but one finds basically the same vision developed in a far more theologically responsible way in Karl Rahner, for example.[2] Younger theologians, such as Johannes Metz,[3] are continuing the development in an ever more radically eschatological direction. Nor is this in any sense a peculiarly Roman Catholic phenomenon. Metz's thinking, for example, at some points closely resembles that of such recent Protestant writers as Wolfhart Pannenberg,[4]

[1] The most comprehensive and careful effort yet made to show how Teilhardian themes can be organized into a responsible theological synthesis is C. F. Mooney's *Teilhard de Chardin and the Mystery of Christ* (New York: Harper & Row, 1966).

[2] See esp. his "Christology Within an Evolutionary View of the World," *Theological Investigations* (Baltimore: Helicon, 1966), V, 157–92.

[3] Three essays illustrating this aspect of his thought may be cited: "The Church and the World," in *The Word in History*, ed. T. P. Burke (New York: Sheed & Ward, 1966), pp. 69–85; "The Controversy About the Future of Man," *Journal of Ecumenical Studies*, IV (1967), 223–34; and "Gott vor uns statt eines theologischen Arguments," *Ernst Bloch zu ehren*, ed. S. Unseld (Frankfort on the Main: Suhrkamp Verlag, 1965), pp. 227–41 (in English, *Cross Currents*, XVIII [1968], 295–306).

[4] The similarities are most apparent in "Der Gott der Hoffnung," in *Ernst Bloch zu ehren*, pp. 209–25 (in English, *Cross Currents*, XVIII [1968], 284–95).

Jürgen Moltmann,[5] and Gerhard Sauter,[6] and has strong similarities (together with crucial differences) to that of Harvey Cox.[7] Further, as English-speaking theologians, we cannot help being reminded of parallel, though independent, efforts to utilize the categories of process philosophy in theological construction[8] even though these latter efforts have as yet had little impact in circles (e.g., Roman Catholic or Lutheran) which take seriously biblical exegesis and the dogmatic tradition of the church.

It is difficult to describe this vision as it is influencing Catholic thought because so far it has not been comprehensively and systematically formulated. This, however, should not lead us to underestimate the importance of its impact on Vatican II. The participants were deeply interested. The thinking of large numbers of bishops and theologians on these matters advanced enormously from 1962 to 1965 during the Council's four sessions. There is evidence for this in some of the documents which were produced and in a good many of the bishops' speeches, but even more in the formal and informal discussions surrounding the official plenary sessions. It is symptomatic that in these no recent thinker was discussed more frequently and more favorably than Teilhard

---

[5] "Die Kategorie *Novum* in der christlichen Theologie," in *Ernst Bloch zu ehren*, pp. 243–63. Cf. also Moltmann's *Theology of Hope* (London: SCM Press, 1967).

[6] *Zukunft und Verheissung* (Zurich: Zwingli Verlag, 1965). As Sauter himself remarks (p. 80, n. 3) in reference to Moltmann, his themes are similar but his approach quite different.

[7] *The Secular City* (New York: Macmillan Co., 1965). Cox fails to affirm the realistically future consummation of all things, yet (rather inconsistently, perhaps) he speaks of the whole of history as the arena in which God is preparing for the coming of the kingdom. Further, as will be indicated later, there is nothing in the view which we are describing which demands Cox's uncritical celebration of modern urban, technological civilization.

[8] E.g., Archbishop William Temple, *Nature, Man and God* (London: Macmillan & Co., 1934); L. S. Thornton, *Revelation and the Modern World* (London: Dacre Press, 1950); Daniel D. Williams, *God's Grace and Man's Hope* (New York: Harper & Bros., 1949); John Cobb, *A Christian Natural Theology* (Philadelphia: Westminster Press, 1965), and its sequels. While it may be possible to utilize some Whiteheadian process motifs in the development of a realistically eschatological outlook such as we are describing, this has not yet been done. A process theologian for whom the second coming of Christ and its prolepsis in the resurrection are of central importance has not yet emerged. Traces of interest in such a program can, however, be seen in John Cobb, "A New Trio Arises in Europe," in *New Theology*, ed. M. E. Marty and D. G. Peerman (New York: Macmillan Co., 1965), II, 250 ff.

de Chardin. Even theologians who had never mentioned him in print and who insisted that he was a poor theologian found his ideas enormously suggestive.[9]

In trying to characterize this vision in more detail, it is necessary to contrast it with the theological framework of thought which it is replacing. This might be described in brief as the nature-supernature version of the classical world view. For the sake of brevity, we shall call it the "classical" or "Christianized classical" view, in contrast to the newer "eschatological" or "realistically eschatological" one.

One of the commonest ways of describing the classical theological view is to say it had a "two-storied"—or, sometimes, "three-storied"—picture of the world. The lowest level is the realm of time and matter, or, more broadly, of nature in general. Above is the immaterial domain of angels, of heaven, and of created supernatural realities. At some unlocated point beyond is the infinite God himself (who, to be sure, because of his omnipotence, omniscience, and omnipresence, is also immanent in the created order).

There is an almost irresistible tendency in this context to think of human beings dualistically. Man, as John Donne phrased it, is an amphibian, composed of material body and immaterial soul, fluttering wretchedly between the first and second levels. The Christian also is an amphibian, living half in the realm of fallen nature and half in that of supernatural grace. Even the Aristotelian anthropology of St. Thomas Aquinas with its emphasis on the soul as the form of the body does not successfully resist this imagery. The notion of the "ghost in the machine," as Gilbert Ryle has named it,[10] still continues to dominate the imaginations of theologians as well as of laymen. It still supplies the pictures with which most Christians think, at least in church on Sundays, even if not during the rest of the week. It is deeply embedded in

[9] This is my impression on the basis of many conversations during the three sessions I was in attendance at the Council as a delegated observer. Evidence from the documents will be introduced later. As for the discussions in the Council aula, Cardinal Meyer (of Chicago) gave a speech on Oct. 20, 1964, which may be cited as a good example (briefly reported in *Council Daybook, Vatican II, Session 3* (Washington: National Catholic Welfare Conference, 1965), pp. 164–65.

[10] G. Ryle, *The Concept of Mind* (London: Hutchinson, 1949).

most discourse on religious matters, in the liturgy, theology, and devotional writings. It influences the way Christians feel and act, nourishing that otherworldliness, that sense that religion is peripheral, having little to do with real life on this earth, which so many now think is one of the major problems of Christianity in our day.

Correlated with this dualism of the spiritual and the unspiritual, the sacred and the profane, is individualism. Salvation in this classical outlook is visualized as a matter of individual souls escaping one by one from the lower level of time and matter into heaven above. A self-centered preoccupation with the salvation of one's own soul has been given support by the way even theologians portrayed reality as a whole.

This two-storied, nature-supernature pattern of thought is ancient, originating so early in Christian history that it is still often automatically identified with Christianity itself. It began developing as soon as the gospel encountered Greek thought, and traces of it are to be found, some exegetes say, even in the later books of the New Testament.[11] The Greek picture, we recall, was of a static universe composed of the domains of being and becoming. Even on the level of becoming, there was no real history or development. The fundamental structures of the physical world, the types of animal species, and the patterns of human life all remained unchanged from eternity to eternity. Or if there were large-scale changes, as the Stoics, for example, believed, these were conceived as cyclical repetitions in which, after vast lapses of time, the very same events began happening all over again.

We are all aware of how utterly antithetical this was to the Bible, which pictures the world not in terms of endless sameness but as the story of God's creative and redemptive action and man's ever new responses. For the Bible, the great divide is not the vertical ontological contrast between material and immaterial, natural and supernatural but the horizontal, temporal contrast between the two ages of the same world's history. The new age has begun in Christ, even though it still remains partly hidden, and

[11] E.g., E. Käsemann, "An Apologia for Primitive Christian Eschatology," *Essays on New Testament Themes* (London: SCM Press, 1964), pp. 169–95.

salvation, though intensely personal, is not individualistic, for it is mankind and the cosmos as a whole which are being redeemed, and men are saved by entering into the new humanity. Instead of being a never-finished tale told by an idiot signifying nothing, the earth and human history have a goal, a purpose, a climactic consummation, when this world, the concrete world of our experience, will be restored, transformed, and united through Christ with God (Acts 3:21; Rom. 8:19–22; Eph. 1:10; Col. 1:20).

We cannot criticize the early Christians or the generations which have followed them for eighteen hundred years for weakening this biblical eschatological vision. They preached the gospel in a Greek milieu to people for whom Hebraic categories were alien and unintelligible. Indeed, through most of history, when the Gentiles in the church have tried to be realistically eschatological, they have literalized and trivialized the messianic expectations in such a way as to fall into chiliastic and millennialistic heresies, or, in the case of certain types of liberal social gospel, they have become shallowly optimistic Pelagian affirmers of human progress.

Two things happened when the early Fathers of the church interpreted the faith in terms of the classical framework. Greek thought was Christianized, but Christian thought was also Hellenized. We see the Christianization of Greek thought in the Fathers' insistence that the world had a beginning and an end, that certain events such as the fall into sin, the covenant with Israel, and the incarnation were utterly unique, never-to-be-repeated. We have already noted some of the results of Hellenization. The physical universe and secular history were viewed not as the world which God loves and redeems but as the religiously unimportant background for God's saving work in the hearts of individuals. The coming of the kingdom of God was no longer the hoped for redemption of humanity and the cosmos, but was viewed exclusively in terms of final judgment, the total destruction of almost everything except the souls of the redeemed and, oddly enough, their resurrected bodies. Through most of Christian history the resurrection has not been the vivid focus of hope for the world's salvation; rather, it has been an uncomfortable addendum to theological treatises. One sometimes suspects it would have been cheerfully sacrificed in favor of an exclusive emphasis on the soul's natural immortality if it had not been for the clear testimony of Scripture.

There have been many versions of the Christianized classical world view. Not all of them have all the features we have mentioned. For example, the technical theological distinction between the natural and the supernatural was not fully elaborated until the time of Aquinas. Further, it was rejected by the Reformation tradition. Yet even this tradition remained heavily indebted to such earlier forms of Christian classicism as that of St. Augustine. Those theologians who have been consciously opposed to the classical Greek view have often retained its anthropological dualism and individualism in disguised forms. They see creation simply as the sphere in which God intervenes from time to time in order to produce saving faith in the privacy of the single soul, and fail to understand it as that which God is directing towards its consummation. Even modern existentialists often do this with their disregard of the objectivities of history and the social dimension of human life. They sometimes seem to replace the ontological distinction between two metaphysically opposed types of being with an equally timeless distinction between the realms of authentic and inauthentic existence. This is particularly evident when Schubert Ogden,[12] for example, presents Jesus Christ as the actualization of a permanently available possibility of life.

But in criticizing the classical Christian outlook we should remember that many of its proponents are completely orthodox in the sense that they strive to express to the best of their ability the wonders of God's revelatory word. To be sure, their categories and language are inevitably time-conditioned and inadequate, but they were often immensely effective and relevant. Spiritualism and Platonic idealism in the case of St. Augustine, or the concentration on individual inwardness characteristic of Pietism, were meaningful in their day. They had a profound influence even on earthly realities, as is witnessed by the transformations of culture and society to which they contributed.

[12] *Christ Without Myth* (New York: Harper & Row, 1961), pp. 160–63; cf. also his *The Reality of God* (New York: Harper & Row, 1967), esp. pp. 164–230 *passim*.

However, the proponents of a realistically eschatological vision are inclined to argue that in our present situation this spiritualism, idealism, and concentration on individual piety are losing all contact with what men now think and feel as reality. This is the atom of truth in the God-is-dead theologies. The supernaturalistic deity of Christianized classicism is dead; but the Christian will continue to affirm that the God of Abraham, Isaac, and Jacob, and of his Lord Jesus Christ, is forever the sovereign master and redeemer even when he veils his face and withdraws the sense of his living presence from us.

This is not the place to describe at length the modern world view, the often unconscious habits of thought and feeling in terms of which we grasp reality. Briefly, we can say, first, that it involves a much more intense awareness of man's intrinsically social character and the conviction that the network of I-thou relationships into which we grow constitutes us, in one fundamental sense, as human beings. Second, the psycho-physical unity of the self is now seen as much more than the abstract metaphysical truth that it was for the Aristotelians; instead, it controls all thinking about human life except, unfortunately, when we are in church. Third, the world in which human beings live is increasingly man-made, and the sense of an immediate relationship and dependence on the natural environment has receded. Nature is not experienced as the divine or the reflection of the divine, but is rather looked at as matter to be manipulated and dominated. The world, in short, has been secularized. Fourth, and most important for our present purposes, modern men, Christian and non-Christian, picture the cosmos in which we live as a unified developmental evolutionary historical process which had a beginning and will have an end, in which new things are constantly happening with ever accelerating speed, and which seems to be going someplace even though it is quite beyond the possibility of empirical, scientific prediction to say where.

The religious implications of this are immense. That which transcends the reality we experience and know is no longer thought of, as it was in the two-storied, non-historical universe, in terms of a realm of timeless truth, value, and beauty above us or within us (the latter is what Paul Tillich holds). Rather, that which transcends the world of our experience lies ahead in the undecipherable possibilities for good and evil into which humanity finds itself hurled with ever increasing speed. Our contemporaries are not likely to encounter transcendence as something discontinuous with the human world of history, as something entered by escaping out of time into the relative timelessness of nature or the total timelessness of eternity. Rather, they meet it as the unknown future towards which mankind and the universe are rushing.

This is the specifically modern experience of transcendence. Of course, it does not exclude other encounters with the unfathomable mystery which surrounds us, such as that which comes to every man in death. However, vast numbers of our contemporaries do not seem to have, or do not consciously articulate, any so-called "religious experiences" whether of a modern or a traditional type. Part of the process known as secularization is the vast increase of practical, even more than of theoretical, atheism. The sense of transcendence appropriate to pretechnological cultures or to a two-story outlook is vanishing—and with it the relevance of theological constructions and modes of piety which developed within those frameworks.

When our situation is viewed in these terms, the fundamental theological response to these new problem areas is to be seen in the revival of biblical eschatological thinking. This revival has in part been prompted by modern scholarly research, itself correlated with the historical perspective, which has made clear how radically unbiblical was the classical framework of nearly two thousand years of Christian thought. But biblical eschatology is not gaining ground only because theologians think they should be faithful to the scriptural witness. This does play an important part. Its success, however, is to be attributed mostly to the fact that the eschatology of the New Testament makes sense in the modern framework in a way that it could not in the classical outlook. As a consequence, it no longer needs to be banished to a kind of postscript in the theological manuals and in Christian spirituality. It can move once again into the center. Hope, anticipation, and openness for the future salvation which God is preparing for the world as a whole can once again become an essential dimension and mainspring of Christian faith and love.

This renewed emphasis on eschatology has not generally issued in attempts to provide a biblical-eschatological interpretation of the modern world view. It has not, in the terminology we have used, been "realistic," but has rather existentialized eschatology (cf. Bultmann), or has followed a two-story pattern of thought by making *Heilsgeschichte* quite distinct from world history (cf. Cullmann).[13] The realistic eschatology which we are describing does not so much reject these other formulations as go beyond them. It agrees fully with their emphasis on the personal and existential dimensions of faith. Indeed, it is hard to imagine any authentic recovery of biblical eschatology which fails to do this. The New Testament stresses that the whole man to the very depths of his being is confronted with the necessity to decide for or against the future, for or against the New Age which began in Christ and will be consummated at his return. The cry, "Repent, for the kingdom of God is at hand," stands at the very center of the gospel. However, those whose eschatology is not realistic generally tend to ignore everything except this personal-existential emphasis. They tend to ignore or demythologize the objective cosmic images through which the biblical writers expressed their faith and hope in God's future transformation of this concrete world in which we live into a new heaven and a new earth.

In contrast, the realists retain these themes and are interested in trying to show how through them one can give a genuinely Christian interpretation of the modern historical-developmental world view. This world, they suggest, in its very physical reality will be transformed into the kingdom of God which has begun in Jesus Christ. All that is pure, honorable, and of good report, whether it develops within the explicitly Christian sphere or not, whether it is specifically religious or apparently secular in character, will enter into the final consummation. Some versions of this view insist that genuine human advances of all sorts have eternal value. The course of earthly history and the worldly tasks

---

13 Oscar Cullmann discusses his own views in contrast to those of Bultmann and his successors in *Salvation as History* (New York: Harper & Row, 1967).

which necessarily occupy the attention of most men most of the time are not simply a meaningless background to spiritual realities, but enter into their very constitution.

This is not at all the same as an immanentism which substitutes evolution, creative or otherwise, for God. The final manifestation of the kingdom will not be an earthly achievement. It will burst disjunctively into history from above just as it began in Jesus Christ, not as an emergent novelty, but as God's transcendent act. Yet, according to such applications of eschatology to the modern world view, God is now guiding all the processes of nature and history in preparation for the fulfillment just as all history before Christ was preparation for Him who came in the fullness of time and as the fulfillment of all times. The early Fathers thought of even Greek philosophy and the Roman peace as part of the *praeparatio evangelica,* as necessary, though by no means sufficient, conditions for the coming of the Messiah. Similarly, this newer outlook views human history and human progress in all their ambiguities as part of God's plan for the world, as part of the *praeparatio eschato-logica.*

This end of history cannot, of course, be imagined or described. It can be represented only in pictures or symbols whether they be those of the Apocalypse or, in our day, the perhaps equally non-literal scientistic imaginings of a Teilhard de Chardin. Yet that end and that fulfillment are real. The statements which affirm it are believed in faith to be propositionally true in the empirically, even though eschatologically, verifiable sense which modern analytic philosophy makes a condition for genuine assertions.[14]

This vision of a universe in movement towards the Eschaton has made extremely rapid progress in Roman Catholic circles in the last few years. It has more affinities with certain traditional Catholic emphases than with Protestant ones[15] simply because it

---

[14] The notion of "eschatological verification" has been used by John Hick, *Faith and Knowledge* (Ithaca, N. Y.: Cornell University Press, 1957); and by I. M. Crombie, "Theology and Falsification," in *New Essays in Philosophical Theology,* ed. A. Flew and A. MacIntyre (New York: Macmillan Co., 1955), pp. 109–30.

[15] This statement holds true of mainstream "orthodox" Protestant theology and of Pietism, but not of those groups coming from the "left-wing" Reformation and from Calvinism which put strong emphasis on the earthly coming of the kingdom, nor of the nineteenth-century liberals with their attempts to

also speaks in objective terms and does not confine itself to personalistic and existentialist categories. It can even be made to appear as an historicized and eschatological version of certain emphases of St. Thomas Aquinas (e.g., that grace does not destroy but perfects nature, or that the soul is the form of the body).[16] Nevertheless, it is fundamentally different from the sixteenth-century scholasticisms to which the Reformers objected. Consequently the old criticisms simply do not apply. It represents an approach which Protestants can adopt and, indeed, as we have noted, a number of them are working independently along lines which parallel this Roman Catholic thinking.

However, it is probably true that most Protestants are sharply opposed to this kind of objective eschatology. They prefer versions which are more exclusively concerned with the present and personal reality of the Eschaton. No doubt this is partly because Protestant theologians have painful memories of the evolutionary optimism of nineteenth-century liberalism. Consequently they are intensely suspicious of efforts to relate the concrete social, political, and intellectual developments of history to God's kingdom even when these efforts stress the transcendent and even apocalyptic aspects of the kingdom far more than the social gospel ever did. However, there are also objections based on reason, and others which are based on faith.

As far as reason is concerned, many theologians apparently think that modern man cannot conceive of history ending objectively in any other way than that suggested by the scientists when they speak of the explosion or extinction of the sun, the operations of the second law of thermodynamics, or the collapse of an oscillating universe. However, when one thinks of the appeal of science fiction, of Marxist utopian myths, or of Teilhard de Chardin, one becomes wary of dogmatizing about what modern man can or cannot believe. It is doubtful, contrary to what many academic

synthesize Christianity and evolution. Cf., e.g., H. R. Niebuhr, *The Kingdom of God in America* (Chicago: University of Chicago Press, 1937); and E. Benz, *Evolution and Christian Hope* (New York: Doubleday & Co., 1966).

[16] P. Chauchard, *Man and Cosmos* (New York: Herder & Herder, 1965), represents a clumsy effort to synthesize a Teilhardian position with Aquinas. Karl Rahner's work as a whole, in contrast, is a skillful attempt to develop a contemporary version of Thomism.

theologians seem to think, that we are moving into a period when world pictures are less necessary and less mythical (though, to be sure, the myths must now be related to science) than in the past.[17] Even on a less imaginative level, process philosophy of the White-headian type illustrates that men whose *Weltbild* is thoroughly modern retain the possibility of thinking of history as ending objectively in a new realm of being, not in annihilation.

These considerations should not be made the basis of a questionable apologetics which tries to prove that Christian eschatological hopes are "reasonable" from the viewpoint of modern secularism. They remain just as incredible as was the resurrection to the Greeks whom Paul addressed on the Areopagus (Acts 17:32). But these hopes become vastly more vivid and compelling when they are related to the new vision of the world. They become hopes not for some shadowy otherworld but for this world in which we think, feel, and live. Even while remaining wildly improbable, they become meaningful in the present situation, just as the early Christian articulations of these same hopes were both meaningful and improbable to the inhabitants of the two-story universe.

Another difficulty with this kind of realistic eschatology is more specifically theological, and for our purposes, therefore, more serious. Existentialists claim that any kind of "objectivizing" thought is dangerous for faith. It threatens to substitute belief in what purport to be factual statements about the end of the world for that radical risk of decision and total openness to God's future, which are the essence of biblical eschatology and Christian faith. After all, so the argument goes, the heart of the New Testament message is concerned with man's decision in the present for or against the New Age which has begun in Christ. Nothing can be allowed to distract from this. What does the future redemption of humanity profit a man if he lose his soul here and now?

The Reformation provenance of this kind of objection is evident. It is a transposition into a modern idiom of the *sola fide*. However, it is at the same time obvious that the sixteenth-century

---

[17] The socio-psychological arguments for this point are summarized in H. A. Murray (ed.), *Myth and Mythmaking* (New York: Braziller, 1960); cf. esp. the Introduction.

Reformers did not have the distaste for objectivities of so many of their modern disciples. They believed that historical faith (e.g., intellectual assent to the objective truth of the resurrection and the future judgment) was involved in saving faith (i.e., *fiducia*). For them, as is quite clear from the Lutheran confessional writings, the distinctive Reformation emphases, such as justification by faith alone, were necessary correctives of the distortions which had crept into the tradition and not at all meant to be constitutive of a basically new understanding of Christianity as many contemporary Protestants suppose. There can be no doubt that while those who reject eschatological objectivity are more insistent on what is specifically Protestant, those who accept it are more faithful to the total thinking of the Reformers which, after all, remained basically catholic.[18]

In short, what I have called the objective version of the eschatological-historical outlook transcends the confessional boundaries. It is neither specifically Roman Catholic nor Protestant, and it provides a new common framework for the discussion of the traditional differences in a way which a purely existential theology, for example, cannot do.

We now have some notion of what is meant by the new vision of the world which provides the new framework for theological thought. It is not formally and explicitly dominant in the Council's documents, but once one is alerted to the contrast between it and the classical outlook one notices evidences of its influence everywhere.

One of the strongest indications of this is the negative fact that only rarely in the hundred thousand words which the Council produced is the classical distinction between the natural and the supernatural introduced. The pattern of thought is sometimes present, perhaps particularly in the Declaration on Religious Freedom, but not once are the terms themselves used in the major documents.

Instead, the Council usually speaks the language of *Heilsges-*

---

18 This general way of understanding the Reformation is developed at length in J. Pelikan, *Obedient Rebels: Catholic Substance and Protestant Principle in Luther's Reformation* (New York: Harper & Row, 1964).

chichte. The church and its mission as well as the coming of Christ are described chiefly in the context of the history of salvation rather than of a two-story universe. To be sure, this can be done even where the basic outlook remains classical; this is illustrated, for example, by St. Augustine's *City of God.* But Vatican II has moved beyond such a position. At certain crucial points it quite clearly affirms that the story of salvation is not a kind of meta-history unrelated to the ordinary course of events. Rather, God is leading the universe in all its aspects, including the so-called secular ones, towards the consummation.

The first of what are perhaps the two most important passages in which this emerges is found in the Council's doctrinally fundamental document, the Dogmatic Constitution on the Church. The seventh chapter, which deals with the eschatological nature of the church, speaks in terms of the contrast between the new and the old aeons. It contrasts the "period between the times" in which we now live with the "restoration of all things" towards which we move. "Then the human race as well as the entire world, which is intimately related to man and achieves its purpose through him, will be perfectly re-established in Christ. . . . In the Church . . . we learn through faith the meaning, too, of our temporal life, as we perform, with hope of good things to come, the task committed to us in this world. . . . The final age of the world has already come upon us. The renovation of the world has been irrevocably decreed and in this age is already anticipated in some real way" (art. 48).

It should be added that this passage is followed by a reversion to the classical perspective in which the horizontal-temporal contrast between the new and the old is replaced by the ontological-vertical distinction between higher and lower realities, between heaven above and earth beneath, between the celestial and terrestrial church. The hope for the restoration of the world as a whole is replaced by the traditional exclusive concentration, characteristic of both Catholics and Protestants, on salvation as the escape of individual souls from earth into transcendence. This is then followed by a carefully guarded but still wholly traditional exposition of the Catholic doctrines of the invocation of the saints and the communion of those below with the saints on high (arts. 49–51). I do not mean that the two parts logically contradict each other. There is consistency of style, for the paragraph which is most thoroughly individualistic remains biblical in its language (art. 48, *fine*). Nevertheless, this is an excellent illustration of that juxtaposition of new and old approaches which we shall find is characteristic of the Council as a whole and which marks it as transitional between two theological epochs.

The most vivid and extended expression of a realistic eschatology is found in the Council's Pastoral Constitution on the Church in the Modern World. This document explicitly acknowledges that "the human race has passed from a rather static concept of reality to a more dynamic, evolutionary one" (art. 5). In speaking of the worldwide increase of "human interdependence" and the growing demand for a social order consonant with "human dignity" for all, it says that "God's Spirit, who with a marvelous providence directs the unfolding of time and renews the face of the earth, is not absent from this development. The ferment of the gospel, too, has aroused and continues to arouse in man's heart the irresistible requirements of his dignity" (art. 26). Finally, it describes our Christian hope in remarkably this-worldly terms.

[Although we do not] know how all things will be transformed . . . we are taught that God is preparing a new dwelling place and a new earth where justice will abide, . . . all that creation which God made on man's account will be unchained from the bondage of vanity.

Therefore, while we are warned that it profits a man nothing if he gain the whole world and lose himself, the expectation of a new earth must not weaken but rather stimulate our concern for cultivating this one. For here grows the body of a new human family, a body which even now is able to give some kind of foreshadowing of the new age.

Earthly progress must be carefully distinguished from the growth of Christ's kingdom. Nevertheless, to the extent that the former can contribute to the better ordering of human society, it is of vital concern to the kingdom of God.

For after we have obeyed the Lord, and in His Spirit nurtured on earth the values of human dignity, brotherhood and freedom, and indeed all the good fruits of our nature and enterprise, we will find them again, but freed of stain, burnished and transfigured. This will be so when Christ hands over to the Father a kingdom eternal and universal: "a kingdom of truth and life, of holiness and grace, of justice, love and peace." On this earth that kingdom is already present in mystery. When the Lord returns, it will be brought into full flower. (art. 39)

Not since the early days of the church, perhaps since Irenaeus, has the mainstream of the Catholic tradition spoken in such realistically eschatological terms of a universe which is heading not towards total destruction, not towards annihilation, but towards cosmic redemption. In succeeding chapters we shall observe how this new conceptual framework is related to what the Council says about various aspects of the church and its mission.

2

THE CHURCH'S
SECULAR MISSION

Correlated with the new view of the world discussed in the previous chapter is a new vision of the church. It is shared in its various versions by many Protestants as well as Catholics, and it finds extensive, though fragmentary, expression in the Council's documents.

Briefly, this vision is that of the church as the messianic pilgrim people of God, the sacramental sign (or, as a Protestant might be more inclined to say, "witness") to the kingdom which has begun and will be consummated in Christ. The picture this evokes has two aspects that shape the way in which, first, the nature and, second, the mission of the church are seen. The nature of the church is understood in terms of a pilgrim people. The church is a band of men and women traveling towards the promised land: God's kingdom of justice, righteousness, peace, and love. As they travel towards this goal they are stained with the dust of the journey, frequently weary, bedraggled and complaining, inclined to forget their destination and tempted to turn aside and settle down, yet repeatedly impelled by their memories and hopes to press forward. Second, however, this pilgrim people has a mission. It exists not for itself, but in order to be a concrete witness to the world, a sacramental sign and anticipation in all that it is and does, to Christ and to the kingdom. Apart from this mission, there is nothing which differentiates this people from other peoples.

The whole being of the church, therefore, is mission. It is a sign and witness to the New Age, not only by its words (the worship and preaching which constitute its *leitourgia*), but also by its "secular" service of the world (its *diakonia*), and by the quality of its communal life (its *koinonia*).[1]

In this chapter we shall deal with the church as the pilgrim people of God and with its secular service, its *diakonia*, reserving consideration of the other aspects of the church's mission for later. However, in order to understand the significance of the new, we must as usual compare it with the old. So we shall first remind ourselves of how the church tends to be pictured within the framework of the classical world view.

I

There are many different ways of understanding the church (or anything else, for that matter) within any given world view. World views are influential, but they are by no means completely determinative of the way we think. They can be filled with many different kinds of content. Different theological positions and philosophical options existed within the classical outlook and continue to exist within the modern one. The ideas of an Augustine, of a St. Thomas, or of a Luther still remain vital, and even so completely a classical thinker as Plato has greatly influenced the process philosophy of Alfred North Whitehead. But in each case the older views are reinterpreted, sometimes radically, when placed within the new context.

The same is true of the way Christians think about the church. As far as Roman Catholics are concerned, they have not surrendered their traditional dogmas, even though these are now being interpreted in new ways. Similarly, the notion of pilgrim people was sometimes applied to the church even by those whose thinking was thoroughly classical. But when this concept was used it was used in a different way and not in an eschatological context.

[1] This chapter deals with *diakonia*, chapter three with *leitourgia*, and chapters four and five with various aspects of *koinonia* (unity) viewed chiefly in terms of ecumenism.

One major Catholic way of picturing the church within the classical framework is as the hierarchical institution of salvation, hovering between heaven and earth, half human and half divine, which funnels down from the supernatural level the grace individual men need in order to rise upward.[2] One might say that this is simply the juridical and institutionalized version of those views that stress the heavenly aspect of the church. These are found, for example, in the Pseudo-Dionysian view of the church on earth as a participation in the "celestial hierarchies" or in St. Augustine's identification of the church with the city of God, most of which is in heaven. When this ecclesiological vision is made normative, as it was in the Middle Ages and even more by Bellarmine[3] in the seventeenth century, it leads to an immense exaltation of the ecclesiastical institution. The church is identified with the kingdom of God on earth, rather than being thought of as the community which points and strives towards the kingdom.[4] For the artist imbued with such notions, it was natural to represent the church as the ark of salvation, the bark of St. Peter, riding triumphantly over the billows of life, its captain the pope, its crew the bishops, and its cargo the huddled masses of the laity whom they have rescued from the waves.

In one of the Council's most stirring speeches, Bishop De Smedt of Belgium attacked this traditional pattern of ecclesiologi-

---

[2] This is the picture which corresponds to medieval canonical and post-Tridentine "baroque" and "deistic" tendencies in Catholic ecclesiology. Cf. U. Valeske, *Votum Ecclesiae* (Munich: Claudius Verlag, 1962), pp. 9–12, 34, for brief summary statements and the most complete available bibliographies on this topic (as well as on other topics in regard to which Valeske is cited in the following notes).

[3] Robert Bellarmine's identification of the church with the legally and institutionally defined Roman communion became standard in later centuries. See *De conciliis et ecclesia,* Vol. II of *De controversiis,* book 3, chap. 2 (various editions).

[4] The complaint of the Orthodox theologian S. Bulgakov regarding the traditional view is often cited, even by Roman Catholics: "Above all, Catholicism is organization; the church as authority and kingdom, *civitas divina in terrenis.*" "Le ciel sur la terre," in the special number "Die Ostkirche," *Una Sancta,* III (1927), 43. "Official" Catholic theology was subject to this criticism up to the eve of the Council. Thus C. Journet (made a cardinal by Paul VI) wrote in a book specially commended by Pius XII: "We believe that it is impossible to avoid identifying the church and the kingdom. These are two notions, but the same reality. The church is the kingdom and the kingdom the church." *L'église du verbe incarnée* (2d ed.; Paris: Desclee de Brouwer, 1962), II, 997, n. 1.

cal thought because it fostered the vices of juridical institutionalism, clericalism, and triumphalism.[5] It emphasizes juridical and
external institutional structures because these can be most easily
thought of as somehow elevated above the mundane course of
events. Even today, "the church does so-and-so" is generally
thought of as referring to the institution, not only by Catholics,
but by others also. This is in turn associated with clericalism.
"Men of the church" are clergymen, as if the church were composed entirely of them. Ordinary lay members are thought of not
as really being part of the church but as the passive recipients
of the ministrations and guidance of the clergy. Triumphalism is
also supported by this outlook. If the church is so nearly divine,
it can do no wrong. Not only is it so thoroughly imbued with
God's holiness that it cannot sin, but it also partakes of his im-
mutability to the extent that it need not change except in the
most superficial respects. The church is not only to be obeyed,
it is to be adored.

There has long been resistance to such views. Beginning more
than one hundred years ago, some theologians placed more stress
on the spiritual and interior aspects of the church as mystery of
salvation, communion of faith and love, mystical body of Christ.[6]
The traditionalists, however, modified these emphases by placing
them within their own framework. Thus Pius XII's encyclical
Mystici corporis (1943) illustrates that the church as the body
of Christ can be conceived in a thoroughly classical and juridical
way as a divine-human organism bridging the gap between heaven
and earth.[7]

The mission or purpose of the church in this classical perspective is primarily the saving of the individual souls who come

[5] De Smedt's speech was printed in *Le Monde* (Paris), December 4, 1962. It
was only one of many similar criticisms directed by the bishops against the
first draft of The Constitution on the Church. See J. M. Estevez, "The Constitution on the Church: *Lumen Gentium*," in *Vatican II: An Interfaith Appraisal, op. cit.,* esp. pp. 102–8.

[6] In the course of emphasizing these nonjuridical aspects, J. A. Moehler first
developed the notion of the church as the "continuation of the incarnation" (in
1835), but it was not until the period 1920–1943 that a "mystical body" ecclesiology became dominant. See Valeske, *op. cit.,* pp. 196 ff.

[7] *Ibid.,* pp. 217–36.

under its care. On this point, strange as it may seem, the Protestant view has not been wholly dissimilar. To be sure, the hierarchical and institutional aspects of the church are de-emphasized, but still the means of grace (i.e., the preaching of the word and the administration of the sacraments) are looked at in a way analogous to the Catholic view of the ecclesiastical institution. They are seen as God's acts spanning the gap between heaven and earth, conveying salvation to men. Further, even though the Protestants have thought of the church as a product or function of the means of grace, as *creatura verbi,* while the Catholics tended to reverse the relation, still both groups conceived of the task of the visible church primarily as that of providing individuals with access to the sacraments and the word.

Correlated with this view is the assumption that God has given to the church or to the explicitly Christian means of grace a quasi-monopoly of his saving power. Catholic theologians have long held that salvation is possible outside the visible church, but this was thought of as highly exceptional. In the vast majority of cases, salvation was impossible, or, at best, dangerously uncertain, except within the ecclesiastical institution. The desire to save from hell the unnumbered millions of heathen was a major motive of foreign missionary work. Such convictions were also closely related to infringements of religious liberty and insistence on the earthly, visible status and power of the church. External pressure is permissible to protect the ignorant from false teachers. We need mention only the names of St. Augustine, Luther, and Calvin to realize that within the classical framework these conclusions seemed compelling to even the most authentically Christian thinkers. Coercive measures, prompted even if not applied by the church, were regarded as legitimate means of repressing heresy and preventing the simpleminded from escaping from those ministrations through which alone salvation was a real possibility.[8]

---

[8] It should be remembered that early Protestant theories of persecution were sometimes more intolerant than Catholic ones, as was pointed out by Lord (John) Acton in 1862 in his still-famous essay, "The Protestant Theory of Persecution," *The History of Freedom and Other Essays* (London: Macmillan & Co., 1909).

II

We turn now to the new vision of the church as the pilgrim people which is a sacramental sign. This vision of the church is not a deduction from the new view of the world. Rather, it is derived largely from biblical and patristic studies, from the return to the sources of the faith. It is in a sense, therefore, older than the views which are usually spoken of as traditional but which are actually later developments stemming from the Middle Ages and the post-Reformation period. This refurbished patristic and biblical vision of the church is now being revived in a form which is congruent with and receives support from the eschatological version of the modern world view which we described in the first chapter.

This new vision of the church is by no means consistently maintained in the Council documents. It is nevertheless highly influential. The most important of the Council's pronouncements, the Constitution on the Church, uses *heilsgeschichtliche* rather than nature-supernature categories when in the first chapter it describes the church as the mystery and sacramental sign of redemption. The second chapter develops the notion of the church as the messianic pilgrim people of God. It is not until the third chapter, which deals with the hierarchy, especially the pope and bishops, that we encounter the non-eschatological, non-historical categories of the classical outlook. Although it emphasizes the motif of ministerial service, it speaks of the church as if it were primarily the institution of salvation (even though it does not use the term). These three views of the church—as sacrament, pilgrim people, and institution of salvation—are juxtaposed without any clear indication of their systematic priorities or interrelationships. The result is that the constitution is open to both conservative and progressive interpretations, depending on which of the leading ideas is made central and provides the hermeneutical framework and principles for interpreting the rest of the statement.[9] While this ambiguity is frustrating for those who would like to define the Catholic view of the church with precision, it is nevertheless probably fortunate. It reflects the Council's desire to be "pastoral," to make a minimum of doctrinal decisions, and leave room for theological variety and development.

Clearly, those interested in an eschatologically oriented ecclesiology will give pride of place to the image of the messianic pilgrim people.[10] Like any other theological concept, this image can be interpreted in various ways, depending on the hermeneutical framework within which it is set. In a static classical outlook it may simply mean that the Christian's true home is above. When placed in the context of the vast sweep of cosmic and human history as this is understood in our day, however, it evokes the biblical picture of the Israel of God journeying out of the old age into that future which has begun in Christ even though it is not yet fully manifest. The church cannot be identified with the kingdom of God on earth, but rather strains towards the kingdom. It is at most the "germ and the beginning" of the kingdom (C 5), the community in which the hidden though real coming of the Eschaton in Jesus Christ is celebrated and its final manifestation at his return awaited. This people lives in the period between the times when preparation for Christ's Parousia at the end of the ages is much more the *leitmotif* than has traditionally been supposed.

The connotations of this picture of the pilgrim people are momentous. First, it makes it impossible to think of the church as fundamentally an institution, or as consisting primarily of the clergy. Rather, it is the people themselves, the laity, who are the church. Wherever they gather together in faith, in worship, or in action, there the church is present even when its normative institutional features are lacking. This is recognized by the con-

[9] The analysis in this paragraph is developed in more detail in my essay, "The Constitution on the Church: A Protestant Point of View," in *Vatican II: An Interfaith Proposal, op. cit.,* pp. 219–36.

[10] For guidance on the immense literature on this theme, see Valeske, *op. cit.,* pp. 239–44; Y. M.-D. Congar, "The Church: The People of God," in *The Church and Mankind,* Vol. I of *Concilium* (New York: Paulist Press, 1965–), pp. 11–34.

stitution, not only by the enhanced place it gives the laity (chap. 4), but also when it defines the church in terms of the worshiping community (rather than as the community juridically authorized to worship),[11] and when it speaks of Christian groups which do not have hierarchical structures as nevertheless having an ecclesial character.[12]

In the second place, the church can no longer be envisioned as fundamentally immutable or changeless. Because it is a pilgrim people journeying from one epoch to another and from one culture to another, it is seen as deeply involved and affected by the vicissitudes of history, not as skimming lightly over the waves of change. This image of the people fits in with our contemporary awareness that the church is an historically and sociologically concrete community subject in one dimension of its being to the same laws of change as any other society. This is the ecclesiological foundation for that call to constant *aggiornamento*, to constant "updating," which is a major theme of all the Council documents.[13]

Third, the church as the pilgrim people cannot be represented as glorious and faultless to the same degree as when one starts with the notion of the body of Christ or the institution of salvation. Because the people is the church, one cannot speak as glibly as Catholics have done in the past about the church itself being in no way sinful but only having sinners within it. The church can become fixated at an earlier and no longer appropriate stage of its life. It is subject to deviations on its pilgrim road; it can, to some degree at least, long for the fleshpots of Egypt or look backward as did Lot's wife. Lastly, it has not yet arrived

11 This is not a central theme of the Council, but it is suggested in a number of the references to the local church and the worshiping community—most clearly, perhaps, when it is said that "the liturgy is the outstanding means by which the faithful can express in their lives, and manifest to others, the mystery of Christ and the real nature of the true Church *(genuinam verae Ecclesiae naturam)*" (SL 2). Cf. SL 8, 10, 33; C 3, 11, 26; G. Baum, "The Ecclesial Reality of Other Churches," *Ecumenical Theology No. 2,* ed. G. Baum (New York: Paulist Press, 1967), pp. 170–77; and, among Council speeches, especially that of Bishop Schick, *Council Speeches of Vatican II,* ed. H. Küng *et al.* (New York: Paulist Press, 1964), pp. 35–38.

12 E 3, 15, 20–23. Cf. also chap. 4, below.

13 Abbott C. Butler, "The *Aggiornamento* of Vatican II," in *Vatican II: An Interfaith Appraisal, op. cit.,* pp. 3–13.

at the end of its pilgrimage; it is not yet made perfect. All this is implicit in the image of the messianic people when seen in an eschatological perspective, and this provides the basis for the reiterated insistence on the need for renewal. At one point, this even leads the Council to declare that the church is in constant need of purification and is *semper reformanda* (E 6). In doing this the Council appropriated themes which Protestants have thought were their private property. Admittedly, it is never explicitly said that the church has sinned, but the theological foundations for such a confession are clearly present.[14]

So far all Protestants will applaud. However much they themselves may also suffer from the vices of institutionalism, clericalism, and triumphalism, they have long been accustomed to denouncing them. But there is a further aspect of the new vision of the world and the church which creates difficulties for traditional Protestantism as much as for Catholicism. The church and the explicitly Christian means of grace can no longer be conceived as having a quasi-monopoly of God's redemptive activity. The role of the church becomes a much more modest one. Some would feel that its very *raison d'être* is threatened.

The role of the church seems to be diminished in a realistically eschatological perspective because salvation is conceived not individualistically but rather in terms of the redemption of mankind as a whole and indeed of the cosmos. In order to bring about such a stupendous result, God must be guiding all the processes of history towards the goal, not simply working redemptively in and through the church. The people of God is viewed much more than formerly as only one of the instruments of God's saving activity. Contemporary Roman Catholic proponents of this outlook insist that this does not mean there is salvation apart from

---

[14] In the Constitution on the Church it is said that the church is "always in need of being purified (*semper purificando*), and incessantly pursues the path of penance and renewal" (art. 8). It is "wounded by sin" (*peccando vulneraverunt*, art. 11), and the faithful are exhorted "to purify and renew themselves so that the sign of Christ may shine more brightly over the face of the Church" (art. 15). The last quotation implies that what the Council defines as the central function of the church, viz., to be a "sign" of Christ, is impaired by the sins of its members. Cf. the fullest study yet made of this theme by K. Rahner in *L'église de Vatican II*, Vol. 51*b* of *Unam Sanctam*, ed. G. Barauna (Paris: Cerf, 1967), pp. 373–91.

Christ, for it is precisely the *gratia Christi* which is at work preparing for the new humanity in many anonymous ways outside the church as well as explicitly within it.[15] The ever increasing actualization of human potentialities in the course of history is willed by God as preparation for Christ, as preparation for the incarnation and the consummation, and whenever this occurs in genuine openness, in love and trust towards God's future and God's creatures, we must acknowledge the operations of justifying grace. Thus there is no salvation apart from Christ, for one day all the redeemed will confess that it is through him they are saved even though they may not have known it in this time between the times in which we live. The Council has not explicitly affirmed any theory of what Karl Rahner calls "anonymous Christianity,"[16]

[15] This is also the teaching of Vatican II: "God in ways known to Himself can lead those inculpably ignorant of the gospel to that faith without which it is impossible to please Him" (CMA 7). This is the traditional doctrine regarding the possibility of salvation by, in some cases, unconscious desire. It had already been affirmed by the Holy Office in 1949 (DS No. 3870).

[16] See esp. his "Christianity and the Non-Christian Religions," *Theological Investigations, op. cit.,* V, 115–34; and "Die anonymen Christen," *Schriften zur Theologie* (Einsiedeln, Switz.: Benzinger Verlag, 1965), VI, 545–54. Cf. the book-length presentation of Rahner's views on this point by Anita Roper, *The Anonymous Christian* (New York: Sheed & Ward, 1966).

Rahner is mentioned here because he is currently the major Roman Catholic proponent of views which stress the presence of the *gratia Christi* outside the domain of the explicitly Christian. He interprets this as involving a hidden presence of the church (and therefore speaks of "anonymous *Christians*"). On the Protestant side, Paul Tillich's concept of the "latent church" is similar. Some Catholics, however, and most Protestants who (whether in a Barthian or some other way) agree with this emphasis on the universal action of Christ's grace would disagree with this ecclesiological interpretation. For various and varying reasons, they would speak of the presence of the church only where there is articulate profession of Christian faith. What the present book describes as a "realistically eschatological" view of the church agrees with this, and not with Rahner. For a full discussion of current Catholic opinion on this point see F. W. Kantzenbach, "Die Ekklesiologische Begründung des Heils der Nichtchristen," in *Oecumenica 1967,* ed. F. W. Kantzenbach and V. Vajta (Minneapolis: Augsburg Publishing House, 1967), pp. 210–34.

It should be noted that Rahner can appeal to the *extra ecclesiam nulla salus* for his argument that all those who are saved are in some sense part of the church, whether visibly or invisibly. In rejecting such an ecclesiology (on the grounds that it makes biblically unwarranted claims for the church), H. Küng finds it necessary to reject this axiom in its traditional interpretation and to replace it with the positive formulation, "Within the church there is salvation through Christ," together with the personal confession, "For me personally there is no salvation outside the church." He is, as far as I know, the first Roman Catholic author to have made this bold move, thus bringing his ecclesiology (on this point at least) into conformity with a completely realistic eschatological view. See H. Küng, *Die Kirche* (Freiburg: Herder & Co., 1967), pp. 371–78, esp. pp. 377, 378.

but it is strongly suggested by the modesty of some of its statements regarding the church's role. At least four traditional monopolistic claims have been abandoned.[17]

First, neither the church nor "religiousness" itself is the sole avenue to God. There are what may be termed "secular" means of grace. The Constitution on the Church says of atheists, for example, that "whatever goodness or truth is found among them is looked upon by the Church as a preparation for the gospel. She regards such qualities as given by Him who enlightens all men so that they may finally have life" (art. 16).

Second, Christianity has no monopoly on true religiousness. In the Declaration on Non-Christian Religions it is said that adherents of these other religions may be saved, not despite the religions to which they belong but because these religions can truly mediate, however imperfectly, some knowledge and experience of God. They "often reflect a ray of that Truth which enlightens all men" (NCR 2; cf. CMA 9, 11, 21; DR 3, 14; C 16, 17). Therefore, in what seems to be one of the most astonishing statements of Vatican II, Catholics are exhorted "through dialogue and collaboration with the followers of other religions, and in witness of Christian faith and life, to acknowledge, preserve, and promote the spiritual and moral goods found among these men, as well as the values in their society and culture" (NCR 2). This provides at least partial support for the view of some Roman Catholic missiologists that the foreign missionary task of the church may be, on occasion, not to convert Buddhists, for example, but to make them better Buddhists.[18]

In the third place, the church disclaims a monopoly on Christianity, even of truly ecclesial Christianity. In the sentence in the Constitution on the Church which, more than any other, indicates the ultimate doctrinal foundation of Roman Catholic ecumenism, the church of Christ is not exhaustively identified with the Roman communion, but is rather said to "subsist in" it (C 8). Consequently, in the Decree on Ecumenism other Christian

---

[17] Cf. E. Schillebeeckx, *The Real Achievement of Vatican II* (New York: Herder & Herder, 1967), p. 80.

[18] E.g., E. Hillman, *The Church as Mission* (New York: Herder & Herder, 1965).

bodies are acknowledged as having an ecclesial character and as being bearers of Christian values and insights through which even Roman Catholicism can be enriched (E 4, 15). As we shall see in chapter four, these affirmations open up immense ecumenical possibilities. Lastly, as we shall once again mention at greater length in chapter four, the monopolizing of the special gifts of the Spirit by the hierarchy is also being abandoned.

The entire work of the Council could be described from the viewpoint of this surrender of pretensions. Its three most dramatic acts, the Decree on Ecumenism and the Declarations on Non-Christian Religions and on Religious Freedom, all reflect the conviction that Catholics should be respectful, willing to learn, cooperative, and even protectively affirmative towards other religions, churches, and movements, as well as towards individuals outside the church, because God is at work through them also and not only in Roman Catholicism.

III

This brings us to what we have called the secular mission, or *diakonia,* of the church, and to a discussion of its importance within a realistically eschatological perspective. Because the function of the church in all aspects of its life and action is to point to the kingdom of love and justice which has come and is coming, its concrete service of mankind is no less integral a part of its mission and its witness than are its preaching, worship, and communal life. It can function as a full anticipatory sign of the New Age only if it is also concerned about the "this-worldly" aspects of human existence because, as the resurrection affirmed with unsurpassable concreteness, the consummation itself is in a sense this-worldly.

Such an emphasis raises the problems currently debated throughout the Christian world under such names as "religionless Christianity" or "Christian secularism." Our treatment of these will be reserved for the next section when we shall examine how the Council itself relates the traditional "religious" activities of the church to the new emphasis on the secular mission. Here our concern is with this mission itself and, more specifically, with the theological foundations for it sketched by the Council. To what extent has the Council abandoned the classical way of thinking about the church's relation to the secular world in favor of a realistically eschatological outlook?

In the classical framework the church may be deeply concerned with the secular order, but in a way which is likely to be fundamentally conservative or reactionary. It is chiefly interested in promoting a moral, social, and political environment which favors what is thought of as the proper business of the church, viz., the gaining of a large membership or many converts so that as many individuals as possible may have access to the means of salvation contained within the church. From this perspective almost all modern developments are to be deplored. Both democracy and socialism (at least in their European forms) as well as science and industrialism have been associated with the de-Christianization of the West. The masses have wholly or partly escaped from the church's control. The reaction of the Roman Catholic Church to this situation during the last two centuries has been an attempt to preserve its influence on public life either by maintaining the patterns of the past or by forming Catholic ghettos in which the faithful are protected from the acids of modernity. Thus its secular *diakonia* has been largely directed towards building Catholic educational systems, labor unions, political parties, and cultural associations. There has been little Catholic contribution to the "building of the earthly city" as this has taken shape in recent times.

The pessimism regarding the present and future and the nostalgia for the medieval age of faith which this reflects were dominant in large sections of the Roman Catholic Church, including the curia, up to the eve of Vatican II. The Council, however, has abruptly changed this. It emphasized the secular mission of the people of God vastly more than has usually been done in the past. The Church in the Modern World, which is much the longest of its documents, is entirely devoted to this theme. It gives a highly positive evaluation of progress in all realms, not only ethical, social, and political, but also economic, aesthetic, scientific, and technological.[19] Its message is that Christians should throw their energies into the building of the earthly city, and therefore also into their ordinary callings, confident that they can serve God in their daily work just as genuinely as in church on Sundays.[20] They need not suffer from that dreadful schizophrenia which has afflicted so many devout souls who supposed that the secular activities in which they expended the overwhelming proportion of their time and strength were at best of extremely meager importance in the eyes of God. This constitution says: "Earthly progress must be carefully distinguished from the growth of Christ's kingdom. Nevertheless, to the extent that the former can contribute to the better ordering of human society, it is of vital concern to the kingdom of God" (art. 39).

Because our concern is with the broad outlines of the theology of the Council, we shall say nothing here of the details of the social teaching of this document, important though these are.[21]

19 CMW says that modern development, despite its dangers, brings "a more critical ability to distinguish religion from magic . . . [and] superstitions . . . purifies religion and exacts a more personal and explicit adherence to the faith" (CMW 7). "The triumphs of the human race are a sign of God's greatness and the flowering of His mysterious design" (art. 34). "The autonomy of earthly affairs . . . is not merely required by modern man, but harmonizes with the will of the Creator" (art. 36). The church "greatly esteems the dynamic movements of today by which these rights [of man] are everywhere fostered" (art. 41). She "recognizes that worthy elements are found in today's social movements . . ." (art 42). Similar praise is lavished on scientific and technological (art. 57), cultural and aesthetic (arts. 60, 61), and economic (art. 63) advances.
20 The duty of Christians "in no way decreases, but rather increases, the weight of their obligation to work with all men in constructing a more human world. . . . For when, by the work of his hands or with the help of technology, man develops the earth so that it bears fruit and can become a dwelling place worthy of the whole human family . . . he carries out the design of God. Manifested at the beginning of time, the divine plan is that man should subdue the earth, bring creation to perfection, and develop himself" (CMW 57). Cf. CMW 34 for the other major text on this theme.
21 The views expressed are consistently progressive—more or less similar to those which, in the United States, are held by somewhat left-of-center liberal Democrats. This is true of the whole range of themes discussed: the conditional character of the "right to property," the obligation for massive aid to underdeveloped countries, the importance of organizations like the United Nations, the need for disarmament, and the importance of culture and the arts. Only birth control is an exception, and here the Council leaves the door open to future decisions rather than proposing "immediately concrete solutions" (CMS 51, n. 14, in the Latin text). Paul VI's conservatism on birth control is at most reconcilable with the letter, but not the spirit, of Vatican II. There are only two points at which the secular progressivism of the Council falters, viz., in the

In the remainder of this chapter we shall focus on why Vatican II thinks that progress in the "ordering of human society . . . is of vital concern to the kingdom of God."

The Council's answer to this question is in part eschatological, but there is also fragmentarily present another tendency which may be termed "incarnationalist."[22] According to this, the kingdom of God and the body of Christ grow progressively through history. The church will advance until it unifies all humanity and embraces all genuine values of other religions and of secular developments in the fullness of its catholicity. A major way in which this is accomplished is precisely through the participation of Christians in all kinds of secular activities. Thereby they sanctify the world and saturate it with Christian values.[23]

Decrees on Communications and on Education, and in both these cases it is rather moderate versions of traditional Catholic positions which are presented.

In summary, the specific "secular" recommendations of Vatican II follow along the lines already laid down by Pope John's progressive encyclicals, *Mater et magistra* (1961) and *Pacem in terris* (1963). Various conservative positions of the past have been abandoned, and the Roman Catholic Church has now joined what might be called the "Western liberal consensus" (which is also expressed in the pronouncements of the World Council of Churches). This is significant, no doubt, but it scarcely represents a prophetic breakthrough. "The church . . . does not go before mankind as a leader, rather it adapts itself in the essential points . . . to that which many men already recognize as necessary quite apart from having any Christian convictions." E. Schlink, "The Pastoral Constitution on the Church in the Modern World," *Challenge and Response, op. cit.,* p. 175. Because of this, it is not the Council's specific proposals for the solution of the world's problems which are of primary long-range importance, but rather the new theologically based engagement in the world which it recommends.

[22] In this context, "incarnationalists" are those who think in organic terms of some kind of cumulative growth of the kingdom (and/or the church) towards the consummation, while "eschatologists" find it better to picture historical developments inside and ouside the church as "preparing the ground" and (discontinuously and non-cumulatively) "pointing towards" the final manifestation of the kingdom. This corresponds roughly to a distinction which has been customary in Roman Catholic discussions, except that those designated "eschatologists" in the past have generally minimized the theological significance of secular historical developments and the secular mission of the church while, in the present view, these are enormously important as preparation and as witness. Needless to say, eschatological and incarnational motifs are so intertwined in the thinking of many Catholic theologians that it is impossible to locate these theologians neatly in either of these two camps. What we shall describe are "ideal types." For the prior use of this distinction see the article of L. Malavez, "Deux theologies catholiques de l'histoire," *Bijdragen,* X (1949), 225–40; and J. M. Connolly, *Human History and the Word of God* (New York: Macmillan Co., 1965), pp. 155–200.

[23] The specifically secular task of the laity is to "work for the sanctification of the world from within" (C 31), "permeate it by the spirit of Christ" (C 36), "penetrating and perfecting the temporal sphere of things" so that the church,

There are a number of considerations which explain the appeal of this pattern of thought for many of the Council Fathers and which account for its partial incorporation into the documents. The influence of such thinkers as Teilhard de Chardin, with his notion of the "Christification" of the world, certainly played a part.[24] Associated with this was a mood of extreme optimism in certain Roman Catholic circles. The beginning of the renewal of the church generated enormous hopes. There was a widespread expectation that if the church would only become faithful to its mission it would be able to mobilize the forces for good in modern secular developments in order to transform humanity.[25] Further, tactical considerations made it difficult for

"by spreading the kingdom of Christ everywhere . . . might bring all men to share in Christ's saving redemption, and that through them the whole world might in actual fact be brought into relation to Him" (AL 2).

The fullest single expression of the incarnationalist tendency is in the Decree on Missions: "Missionary activity is . . . an epiphany of God's will. . . . Whatever truth and grace are to be found among nations, as a sort of secret presence of God, this activity frees from all taint of evil and restores to Christ its maker, who overthrows the devil's domain and wards off the manifold malice of vice. And so, whatever good is found to be sown in the hearts and minds of men, or in the rites and cultures peculiar to various peoples, is not lost. More than that, it is healed, ennobled, and perfected for the glory of God, the shame of the demon, and the bliss of men. Thus, missionary activity tends toward the fulfillment which will come at the end of time. For by it the People of God advances toward that degree of growth and that time of completion which the Father has fixed in His power." (art. 9)

The "incarnationalism" of this passage is not to be found in the suggestion that all genuine goods and values, whether inside or outside the explicitly Christian sphere, will enter in and find fulfillment in the consummation (such an assertion may also be made from the "eschatological" perspective), but rather in the impression (not, to be sure, clear-cut affirmation) that this happens through the church in such a way that the final manifestation of the kingdom will come as the result of the progressive growth of the church and Christianization of the world. Many other briefer passages give this same impression of a visible growth towards, rather than a *sub contrario* preparation for, the consummation: e.g., "The Church, or, in other words, the kingdom of Christ . . . grows visibly in the world" (C 3).

24 CMW was deeply influenced by Teilhard's positive attitude towards evolution, earthly realities, and modern developments, but not by those particular theses of his which are, according to many, difficult to reconcile with fundamental Christian affirmations regarding the transcendence of God, sin, etc. See O. Spülbeck, "Teilhard de Chardin und die Pastoralkonstitution," and S. M. Daecke, "Das Ja und das Nein des Konzils zu Teilhard," in *Die Autorität der Freiheit, op. cit.,* III, 86–112. This three-volume work is, by the way, much the fullest available collection of texts, Council speeches, and commentaries on the Council from diverse countries, churches, and points of view.

25 For an expression of this attitude, see the exciting and informative account of the first session of the Council by the *Time* correspondent in Rome, R. B. Kaiser, *Pope, Council and World, op. cit.*

the Council to warn against this kind of enthusiasm. The majority was fighting an almost Manichaean version of the classical outlook for which nothing new and nothing outside the church are good. "The prophets of doom," as John XXIII called them,[26] opposed almost all modern developments and called for a wholesale, undiscriminating condemnation of communism, for example. This made it difficult for the Council to warn against excessive optimism regarding Christian social action, or to be critical and balanced in its affirmation of the values of the new, the secular, and the non-Christian. To do so would have seemed a concession to the reactionary pessimists.

The main reason for the appeal of incarnationalism, however, is that, oddly enough, its major premise is traditional. It agrees with the classical outlook in holding that the church should engage in secular *diakonia* because this constitutes a kind of pre-evangelization which contributes to the Christianization of the world and the ultimate triumph of the church. The minor premise and the conclusion, however, are very different. Instead of limiting pre-evangelization to what directly and visibly helps the growth of the church, the incarnationalist thinks of human advances of all kinds as serving this end. He therefore participates fully in the building of the earthly city, confident that this will contribute in the end to the spread of Christianity. Thus a classical first premise combined with a highly optimistic second premise[27] pro-

---

[26] In the opening speech of the Council, reprinted in X. Rynne, *Letters From Vatican City, op. cit.,* pp. 262–72, esp. p. 265.

[27] The major problem is not that the Council speaks too optimistically about the modern world (in view of the need to oppose reactionary nostalgia for the past, this is excusable) but that it is too "optimistic" about the church. The distinction between kingdom and church is not always clearly maintained. The growth of one often appears to be identified with the growth of the other. The recognition of the misery of the church is largely counterbalanced by the assumption (evident in the entire structure of CMW) that the church is, so to speak, "humanity at its best" and is therefore, despite its faults, the best teacher of the world regarding the solution of its problems. The fact that eschatological fulfillment involves judgment is not emphasized, and there is not so much as a suggestion that this judgment also extends to the church. The most unfortunate phrasing is in the Decree on Missions: through the activity of the church, "the Mystical Body of Christ unceasingly gathers and directs its forces toward its own growth," and, at the same time, through this activity, "the plan of God is fulfilled . . . according to which the whole human race is to form one people of God, coalesce into the one body of Christ, and be built up into one temple of the Holy Spirit" (art. 7; cf. arts. 3 and 4). Thus, in the words of one commentator, "the plan of God for the salvation

vides support for greater emphasis on the secular mission of the church. In a way reminiscent of the classical Catholic pattern of grace presupposing and perfecting nature, the incarnationalist understands the Christianization of the world as presupposing and perfecting secular progress and development.

While the church's secular mission is at least as important from an eschatological perspective as from an incarnationalist perspective, it does not, for the eschatologist, depend on this kind of incarnational optimism. The present age is one of "preparation for" not "growth" or "progress" towards the kingdom. There is no guarantee that mankind is becoming better or that the world will be Christianized. All developments are ambiguous and may be used for either good or evil. Such an outlook is more open to the future than an incarnational one. It is less subject to crushing disappointments than are optimistic or utopian views regarding the course of history. No matter what happens, and even if the church's secular mission is not "successful," the church must struggle for love and justice and serve the needs of men because only in this way can it be an authentic anticipation and witness to the final manifestation of God's reign and rule.

As we shall see, this eschatological approach is in general congruent with what the Council says, but it is not fully spelled out. There is little trace of that biblical apocalypticism which is utterly opposed to an evolutionary picture of the kingdom gradually growing through the ministrations of the church until it conquers the world.[28] Similarly, there is only perfunctory atten-

of mankind is seen as being already and only actualized in the growth of the church, and the Christ-given unity of mankind is awaited as the ultimate membership of all in a world church." M. Linz, "Alte Formeln oder neue Erkenntnis," in *Die Autorität der Freiheit, op. cit.,* III, 557. For other presentations of basically the same criticisms, see J. C. Hampe, "Kritische Stimmen zur Theologie der Pastoralkonstitution," in *ibid.,* III, 164–73; P. E. Persson, "Der endzeitliche Charakter der pilgernden Kirche und ihre Einheit mit der himmlischen Kirche," in *ibid.,* I, 338–43; E. Schlink, "The Pastoral Constitution on the Church in the Modern World," *op. cit.;* and, most comprehensively of all, K. E. Skydsgaard, "The Church as Mystery and as People of God," in *Dialogue on the Way, op. cit.,* pp. 145–74. This critique must, however, be balanced by the observation that in some places, especially in the Decree on Ecumenism (art. 7), the Council recognizes its own church's failings more fully than many other ecclesiastical bodies have done.

28 It should be noted that many Roman Catholic theologians do take apocalyptic seriously, even though they "demythologize" its dualistic hostility to the created order in order to make it compatible with the fundamental biblical

tion given to the strange ambiguity of "progress."[29] The corruption of the best is the worst. Advances in every field from nuclear physics to the affluent society create the possibility of unprecedented horrors such as atomic destruction or Orwell's world of 1984. Further, in our contemporary situation, even advances of the thoroughly humane variety which the Council tells Christians to promote do not generally prepare men for the gospel but turn them away, making them more confident of their ability to get along without God. In Bonhoeffer's famous phrase, "the world has come of age," and, whether or not it does in fact need religion, it certainly does not feel that it does.

Thus there are good empirical reasons for believing that Christians will be a minority (a "diaspora") of declining numbers and influence in the foreseeable future.[30] The world will be served by their *diakonia* and witness, but many will be hostile and the church's income and membership may well decline. It is simply impossible to argue persuasively for the church's secular mission, as the incarnationalist tends to do, on the grounds that this is a means of converting the world and making it explicitly Christian.

Further, the Council documents fail to recognize that the major positive contributions of Christianity to human progress have often been made against the will of the churches. They have often fought against that which is good in a scientific, technological, and democratic civilization, even though this is in large measure the product of the biblical faith of which they have been the bearers in history.[31] It was biblical faith that de-divinized nature and

affirmations of the goodness of God's creation and of his lordship over history. E.g., K. Rahner, "Theologische Prinzipien der Hermeneutik eschatologischer Aussagen," in *Schriften* (1960), IV, 401–28.

[29] CMW, to be sure, does call attention to the potentialities for evil in modern developments and the problems raised by human sinfulness (esp. in arts. 4, 5, 8–10, 13). It is indicative of its general tenor, however, that "the first drafters of the schema were so uninhibitedly affirmative regarding the world that they forgot the theology of sin and of the cross and had to insert these later" (in CMW 13). O. Spülbeck, in *Die Autorität der Freiheit, op. cit.,* p. 90.

[30] Once again, Karl Rahner's theological reflections on this theme of the "diaspora" situation of the church are outstanding. An important recent contribution of his is "Konziliare Lehre der Kirche und künftige Wirklichkeit christlichen Lebens," *Schriften* (1965), VI, 479–98.

[31] The most extended theologically oriented discussion of the relationship between biblical religion and Western civilization is that of Arend T. van Leeuwen, *Christianity in World History* (Edinburgh: Edinburgh House Press, 1964).

society, thus freeing men to turn these into material for rational manipulation and advance. Its eschatological hopes have occasioned those upsurges of sectarian, Marxist, and humanistic utopianism and optimism which help make Western civilization a worldwide force inconceivably more dynamic than any other. The church's proclamation that Christ is Lord, faltering though this has been, destroyed the old gods of a static, goalless universe and unleashed the revolutionary forces which are driving mankind forward in its highly ambiguous progress. From a realistically eschatological perspective, this is part of God's will for the world, but the church has often refused to acknowledge his governance of history and has repudiated even its own legitimate offspring.

For example, the Council's Declaration on Religious Freedom rightly says freedom is based on an awareness of human dignity rooted in the biblical revelation. However, it has developed largely in opposition to the church[32] (and not only the Roman church, although this has been the most notable example). Christians have had to learn about this truth of theirs from their enemies. In short, the church has often been on the wrong side. Vatican II implicitly acknowledged this by the way it abandoned positions held in the past, but it proved impossible to say this clearly. Older pious patterns of thought were too strong among the majority, and so the general impression left by the conciliar document is that everything that is good prepares the way for the church and the church brings to perfection everything that is good.

This, however, is not the final word. Eschatological motifs are

---

[32] The opposition of the church to human progress is acknowledged only in reference to science and religious liberty, and in both cases only indirectly. In CMW it is said that "we cannot but deplore" the ignoring of "the rightful independence of science . . . which leads many minds to conclude that faith and science are mutually opposed" (art. 36). A footnote reference to Galileo at this point suggests, without actually asserting, that his condemnation is one of the things to be deplored. In the Declaration on Religious Freedom it is merely said that in "the People of God . . . there has at times appeared a way of acting that was hardly in accord with the spirit of the gospel or even opposed to it" (art. 12). It should be remembered, however, that even such meager admissions, coming from the highest teaching authority, are new, and they have unleashed in some Catholic circles a chain reaction of confessions of the sins of the church against progress. Further, many of the bishops wanted stronger statements. Elchinger of Strasbourg asked for an official rehabilitation of Galileo, and Beran of Czechoslovakia, Barniak of Poland, and Rossi of Brazil requested, in the name of many other bishops, public penitence for the record of the church on religious liberty.

also present, and the Council nowhere tries to decide between them and the more incarnational ones. Its concern is to stress the secular mission of the church rather than to affirm a particular theological foundation for that mission. Consequently, each of the three major themes in the documents which favor *diakonia* can be interpreted either incarnationally or eschatologically.

This is true of the acknowledgment, which we have already noted, that God is working mightily outside the boundaries of the visible church. The Council insists, far more than have previous generations, that the church must cooperate with this action of God; it must work with and even learn from persons and movements which do not bear the Christian label. As the Constitution on the Church in the Modern World emphasizes, the church must "read the signs of the times" (art. 4), it must discern and contribute to what God is doing in history, for instance (to cite the Council's favorite example) in the growing unification of mankind.[33] A corollary of this is that separate Catholic political parties, trade unions, and cultural organizations can no longer be considered better than joint ones. The formation of Catholic ghettos has in principle been repudiated (e.g., CMW 88–90; E 12).

Second, the description of the church as a "sacramental sign," which is fundamental to the first chapter of the Constitution on the Church, stresses the secular mission and is congruent with (even if it does not necessitate) an eschatological outlook.[34] The

---

[33] This is one of the major unifying themes of the Council. The Constitution on the Church starts by saying that the increasing unification of mankind lends "special urgency" to the mission of the church (art. 1), and the same note is struck in arts. 9 and 28, and in many places in CMW, but especially arts. 42–44.

[34] The notion of "sacrament," whether used in a broad sense to apply to the church (and even more fundamentally, to Christ) or in the traditional narrower and properly liturgical sense, is interpreted differently depending on whether it is understood in an "eschatological" or "incarnationalist" framework. In speaking of the Lord's Supper from an eschatological perspective, J. Moltmann draws the contrast thus: "The congregation at the Table is not in possession of the sacral mystery of the Absolute, but is a waiting expectant congregation seeking communion with the coming Lord." *Theology of Hope, op. cit.,* p. 326. Similarly, the church is the efficacious sacramental sign, not of already triumphant grace but of the coming kingdom. In the Constitution on the Church, the concept of the church as a sacrament is used in both contexts, a predominantly incarnationalist one in art. 2, and a more eschatological one in art. 48. If one makes the mistake of assuming that the only interpretation of the church as

church is "in Christ as a kind of sacrament or sign and instrument of intimate union with God and of the unity of the whole human race" (art. 1). This affirms that its mission is to be an efficacious sign of reconciliation between man and God and man and man, and that this mission, this sign-function, embraces its entire being, all that it is, says, and does, whether overtly religious or not. Even though this is not spelled out at this point, this implies that the messianic people witnesses to the kingdom not only by the testimony of its individual members and by its *leitourgia*, its specifically religious activities of worship and proclamation, but also by its *koinonia*, the quality of its communal life, and by its *diakonia*, its secular service of the world. Indeed, the stress in the Council on this *diakonia* suggests that most bishops believed that the church continues to bear witness most effectively when outsiders are impelled to say, "See how these Christians love one another and"—so we must add—"the world."

Third, this emphasis on the secular mission is further reinforced by the Council's thoroughly eschatological teaching that the church must be the humble servant of mankind, not its lord and master, if it is to function as a visibly authentic sign. The Christ whom it manifests is not yet the Triumphant Lord of the Eschaton, as the traditional Catholic *theologia gloriae* has represented him, but rather the Christ who, although he is the resurrected Lord, is still the servant of reconciling love, hungering with the hungry, suffering with the sufferers, and imprisoned with the captives. Thus, one of the most moving passages in the Constitution on the Church says:

Just as Christ carried out the work of redemption in poverty and under oppression, so the Church is called to follow the same path in communicating to men the fruits of salvation. Christ Jesus, "though He

sacrament is an incarnational one, then it becomes difficult to see how a Protestant could approve of the idea. Kantzenbach makes this mistake in criticizing the present author and others in *Oecumenica 1967, op. cit.*, p. 222, n. 40. (His article contains a full critique of the notion of the church as sacrament together with extensive bibliographical references.) I have sketched a view of the church as *sacramentum* which seems to me acceptable from the perspective of the Reformation in "A Protestant View of the Ecclesiological Status of the Roman Catholic Church," *Journal of Ecumenical Studies*, I (1964), 243–70, esp. pp. 260 ff.

was by nature God . . . emptied himself, taking the nature of a slave," and "being rich, he became poor" for our sakes. Thus, although the Church needs human resources to carry out her mission, she is not set up to seek earthly glory, but to proclaim humility and self-sacrifice, even by her own example. (art. 8)

In short, to repeat the phrase which seemed to move the assembled bishops in the Council more than any other, the church is in its essence and must become manifestly "the church of the poor"[35] and the oppressed, not of the rich and the oppressors. Many bishops insisted this should be true not only within each country but also on an international scale. The church should identify itself more with the poor, underdeveloped countries than with the rich, Western, purportedly Christian ones. It must be freed of institutional self-aggrandizement and come to look at its task as that of serving human needs in every form and in every place even when this does not produce new members or wealth or power. To put the point most forcibly, it must serve human needs even when this would not help produce conversions to conscious faith in Christ. It is called to this self-effacement because only in this way can it be an authentic witness to the Lord who triumphs through the cross, through sacrifice. There are ambiguities in the conciliar documents. But when one takes their total impact there is no doubt that they surrender that identification of the service of God with the promotion of the visible church, of the explicitly Christian, to which Roman Catholicism has been even more prone than Protestantism. They do suggest that the secular mission of the church and the secular activities of Christians are important in their own right, not simply as an adjunct to the religious mission.

Yet any full explanation of why or how this is so is lacking. Only occasionally are there glimmerings of the complete realistically eschatological answer as when the Constitution on the Church in the Modern World says that those who "dedicate themselves to the earthly service of men . . . make ready the material of the

---

[35] Y. Congar, *Pour une église servante et pauvre* (Paris: Cerf, 1963). This book explores various dimensions of "the church of the poor" and records some of the enthusiasm which the theme evoked when it was first introduced by Cardinal Lercaro at the first session of the Council.

celestial realm . . . [and] devote themselves to that future when humanity itself will become an offering accepted by God" (art. 38). This suggests that the work of the earthly city is important, not necessarily because it contributes to the church, as the incarnationalist view holds, but because it supplies material for the kingdom at the end of history. Because God is guiding all the processes of nature and of history towards the consummation, his people are called upon to participate fully in his anonymous humanizing activity even when they do not thereby win members or Christianize the world in any overt way.

It seems to me that we may be fairly confident that this type of theological foundation for the secular mission of the church will become more and more prevalent in Roman Catholic thought. Not only is it implied by the present trend towards eschatological realism, but it is supported, as we have pointed out, by the stress on the church as the humble and self-effacing servant of mankind.

This, however, raises in the most acute form the question of the relation of what we are calling the religious and the secular dimensions of the church's mission. If God acts so massively outside the church and in its secular *diakonia,* then what is the importance or necessity of those activities which have always been thought of as the church's chief business? What is the importance of prayer, of preaching, of the sacraments? We shall say something about this in the next chapter when we ask how the Council's teaching on the explicitly Christian aspects of the church's life, and especially its liturgy, is related to the realistically eschatological perspective.

3

LITURGY:
SUMMIT AND SOURCE

The liturgy, according to the Second Vatican Council, is "the summit toward which the activity of the Church is directed; at the same time it is the fountain from which all her power flows" (SL 10).

Both Christian secularists and the sons of the Reformation have difficulties with the traditional Roman Catholic view of worship. It is from the point of view of their questions that we shall examine in this chapter what the Council says about this topic. In the first part, we shall consider chiefly the secularists' problem. If the service of mankind (*diakonia*) is as crucial as the Council itself claims, then what is the place of the religious service of God (*leitourgia*)? *Why* are prayer, preaching, and the sacraments both the summit and the source of the church's life? In the second, third, and fourth parts, we shall turn to the traditional Protestant objections to Catholic worship. *How* should Christians worship? To what degree does the Council contribute to a solution of the problems raised in this area by the Reformers?

Our use of the word "liturgy" will sometimes be broader than that of the Council documents. They employ it to refer exclusively to the "official" worship of the church, that is, the liturgies of the word and sacrament, and the Divine Office which clerics and members of religious orders recite daily. We, however, shall speak of the church's liturgy as embracing all the activities which are normally thought of as "religious." It therefore includes missionary proclamation, "extra-liturgical" devotions ranging from private prayer to public pilgrimages, and also religious education from the catechism class to the seminary insofar as this is a matter of instructing in, and not simply about, the faith. All of these activities profess to be overtly, and not simply anonymously, Christian. They constitute what the man in the street thinks of as the religious, as distinct from the secular, dimensions of the church's life.

I

Perhaps the gravest of the Council's failures is that its own emphasis on secular service threatens that centrality of liturgy and of missionary proclamation which it wishes to affirm. Thus it unintentionally encourages the growth among Catholics of much the same kind of "Christian secularism" which has become rampant among Protestants. The Council never faces this challenge and, indeed, never really acknowledges its existence. It simply fails to see that its own recognition of the pervasiveness and power of the workings of "anonymous grace" undermines the explanations it gives for the importance of explicitly Christian worship and practice.

Three aspects of the Council's position are of interest to us: (1) it rejects traditional warrants for religious activities, (2) tends instead to ground them in the "incarnationalism" with which we have already become familiar, and (3) avoids taking an eschatological approach, despite its use of this approach in other connections. Each of these points needs comment.

The traditional warrants which it rejects are, quite simply, appeals to hope of heaven or fear of hell. It is not for the sake of the individual's salvation that the Council urges "the performance of religious duties" or "preaching to the heathen." This omission disturbed many of the conservative bishops, as was indicated particularly in the third-session debate on the draft version of chapter seven of the Constitution on the Church.[1] They

---

[1] I have in mind particularly the as yet unpublished interventions of Cardinal Ruffini, Patriarch Gori, and Archbishop Nicodemo in the 80th General Congregation, Sept. 15, 1964.

complained that the doctrine of eternal damnation was being replaced by belief in universal salvation.

Literally speaking, this has not happened; but it must be admitted that a realistic eschatology such as that which influenced the Council capitalizes on the universalistic motifs in the letters of St. Paul, for example, particularly Ephesians and Colossians. It is the redemption of the whole cosmos for which Christians hope and long. All responsible Roman Catholic theologians insist that anyone who is properly aware of the dreadful enigma of human sinfulness must grant at least the possibility that any man can eternally separate himself from the love of God. At the same time, so the progressives remind us, we must remember that the mighty and merciful God wills all men to be saved (I Tim. 2:4), and so it ill behooves us to pretend to know whether the possibility of damnation is ever actualized. Hans Urs von Balthasar has argued that dogmatically to affirm its actualization amounts to subverting the gospel, to making bad news part of the good news.[2] Apparently Vatican II agreed. The mood of its documents is reflected in a witticism which circulated widely during the Council to the effect that the existence of hell is indeed a dogma, but that it is not necessary to believe that there is anyone in it. In view of this attitude, it is no wonder that the bishops refrained from recommending the sacraments, church attendance, or foreign missions on the grounds of rescuing souls from perdition.

The grounds which they substituted, however, are not altogether persuasive, perhaps not even to the bishops themselves. We have already mentioned in the previous chapter the tendency to think in incarnational terms of the progressive Christianization of the world. Progress in "anonymously Christian" love and justice is then seen as a kind of pre-evangelization which eventually leads men to explicit faith in Christ. There is little evidence

---

[2] ". . . If this attitude prevails, faith necessarily takes on the aspect of an intellectual, neutral act comprising truths both of salvation and of damnation without any specific commitment to either. . . . Closely allied to this is a smug notion of hope, which would seem to make it an affront to faith to hope for the salvation of all men." "Eschatology," in *Theology Today*, ed. F. Boeckle *et al.* (Milwaukee: Bruce Publishing House, 1965), I, 234. The German original of this volume, *Fragen der Theologie Heute* (1957) was one of the most substantial and influential pre-conciliar statements of newer trends in Roman Catholic theology.

that this occurs, that what is anonymously Christian does have this natural tendency, at least in the present economy of things, to become explicitly Christian.

The Council assumes not only that grace even in its secular forms tends towards overt manifestation in Christian worship, but also that worship is the basic source of this grace and of the works of love it inspires: "Through the sacraments, especially the Holy Eucharist, there is communicated and nourished that charity toward God and man which is the soul of the entire [lay] apostolate" (C 33). In this and many other ways the Council suggests that works of love, justice, and mercy are the spontaneous fruit and overflow of the power received through religious means of grace.

This emphasis on worship as the dynamic source of good works has long been the standard view of most Christians, although they have differed as to exactly what kinds of liturgy are primary (individual or communal, eucharistic or non-eucharistic, formal or informal). Yet its correctness is questionable. Worship often does not lead to works, as St. Paul, not to mention the author of James, was well aware. Time and again the most assiduous cultivation of the sacraments, preaching, Bible-reading, prayer, and "spiritual experiences" has been combined with flagrant moral and social irresponsibility. In our day increasing numbers of both Catholics and non-Catholics are becoming acutely aware of this. They find implausible the neat division between explicitly religious activities as the sources, causes, or means of grace, and acts of love and justice as their fruits. If God is working redemptively everywhere in preparation for the coming judgment and restoration of all things, then action in trustful openness to one's fellow men and to God's future is itself a means of grace, though a "secular" one. Giving a cup of cold water, visiting the sick and those in prison, and freeing the captives can be anticipatory signs of the coming kingdom, for it is thus that men encounter Christ in their neighbors here and now. Indeed, it can be argued that, according to the Gospels, it is these encounters above all which determine a man's eternal destiny (Matt. 25:31–46).

The Council certainly does not assert this in so many words, but its stress on *diakonia* opens the way to such ideas and implicitly casts doubt on its own way of explaining the importance of *leitourgia*. It is not self-evident that it is primarily in the church's worship that "the work of our redemption is exercised" (SL 2), that it is chiefly here that Christ becomes present and we are incorporated into him (SL 6), that "the liturgy is the outstanding means by which the faithful can express in their lives, and manifest to others, the mystery of Christ and the real nature of the Church" (SL 2). On the contrary, is not the essence of the church often most fully and vividly actualized in serving those in need, in rescuing Jews under Hitler, or in concern about war, whether in Vietnam or elsewhere? When done in faith, even implicit faith, such actions seem to be signs which effect the grace they signify no less genuinely than the most authentic proclamation of Christ in preaching and sacramental action.

The crisis represented by these questions is already far advanced in Protestantism, but Roman Catholicism is not exempt. Harvey Cox's book[3] has become immensely popular and the slogans of religionless Christianity and Christian secularism are widespread.[4] Such views are generally antithetical to sixteenth-century works-righteousness, for they oppose using religious activities as ways of saving oneself. Indeed, Christian secularists often maintain that in attacking religion they are simply carrying the principle of justification by faith to its logical conclusion.[5]

Although some Roman Catholic theologians are now in the process of facing this issue of secularism, it is not surprising that the Council failed to do so. A realistically eschatological answer to the Christian secularist derogation of worship is radical, and no Christian communion is as yet prepared to affirm it in all its consequences.

In the last chapter we discussed the radical nature of realistic

---

[3] *The Secular City* (New York: Macmillan Co., 1965).

[4] Catholics, for example, are well represented in the book edited by D. J. Callahan (himself a Catholic layman), *The Secular City Debate* (New York: Macmillan Co., 1966). See also R. L. Richard, *Secularization Theology* (New York: Herder & Herder, 1967).

[5] The secularists believe themselves in agreement with statements such as this from Dietrich Bonhoeffer: "The Pauline question whether circumcision is a condition of justification is today, I consider, the question whether religion is a condition of salvation. Freedom from circumcision is at the same time freedom from religion." *Prisoner for God: Letters and Papers from Prison,* ed. E. Bethge (New York: Macmillan Co., 1954), p. 53.

eschatology in connection with the theological foundations of *diakonia*. Its radicalness lies in its modesty; it makes no great claims for the world-transforming power of Christian *diakonia*. The same holds true for *leitourgia* when seen from a realistically eschatological perspective. It proffers no grand vision of anonymous grace leading naturally, in this period between the times, to manifest Christianity, nor does it have any illusions about the superior efficacy of the church's *leitourgia* to God's other instrumentalities. It has surrendered the triumphalism of fifteen hundred years of Christendom which tried to argue for the importance of word and sacrament on the grounds that they are indispensable to the salvation of individuals or the world.

No, the reason Christian people preach and worship is that they know they are called to witness to God's redemption, to be explicit witnesses and conscious bearers through all the ages of the memory and hope of the Messiah. They know they cannot do this without *leitourgia,* for memory and hope are rooted in liturgical action. Nor can they witness explicitly to all men without preaching to all.

So far their faith instructs them, but no further. They do not know what God will do with their witness.[6] They can be certain of only one thing. God has willed to save the world, not only through anonymous means of grace but also through explicitly Christian means. For it is precisely towards the full manifestation of what is explicitly Christian, when God through Christ will be all in all, that God is leading mankind. However, we cannot always be sure exactly how the Christian presence is preparing the way. During the Middle Ages, it may have done this partly by shaping a professedly Christian society and by helping to create the dynamic, secular civilization in which we live. In the

[6] One view which has gained favor among some Roman Catholics who think in terms similar to what we are calling "realistic eschatology" is that the church acts as the "representative" of all mankind (thus continuing in an analogous way the representative function of Christ). This is in harmony with the "eschatological answer" expounded in the text, although it also goes beyond it. Needless to say, the biblical support for such a position is considerable. See the article and literature cited by J. Ratzinger, "Stellvertretung," in *Handbuch theologischer Grundbegriffe,* ed. H. Fries (Munich: Kösel Verlag, 1963), II, 566–75. Cf. also J. Feiner, "Kirche und Heilsgeschichte," in *Gott in Welt: Festgabe für Karl Rahner,* ed. J. B. Metz *et al.* (Freiburg: Herder & Co., 1964), II, 317–45.

future, as in the early centuries, the Christian presence may possibly prepare the way more by testifying to Christ as a little flock amidst a largely unbelieving and hostile populace. But one thing the Christian affirms: God wills that there be a messianic people which bears articulate testimony to Christ, and through all millennia he will use that testimony to prepare the way for Christ's return, even in the periods when the main course of history seems set in other channels and the liturgy with its unabashed use of "God-and-Jesus language" seems irrelevant to the world's concerns.

There is something reminiscent of the role of Israel in this view. All are called to the coming kingdom, but not all are called to bear witness to it. The witness-bearers of the new covenant are elected not through circumcision and birth as are the Jews but through baptism and the gift of the faith which believes the incredible good news of God's past, present, future, and eternal love in Christ. Once they find themselves clinging to this good news, they cannot escape their sometimes joyous, sometimes heavy responsibility of remembering and proclaiming it in word, worship, and service. From this perspective, however, the church believes at the same time that the grace of Christ can and does work powerfully even in those whom God has not effectively called to explicit faith, to witness-bearing; and so, even while the kerygmatic and sacramental liturgies remain central for its life, it can cooperate joyfully, respectfully, and without anxiety with what God is doing anonymously in the struggle against evil outside its boundaries, outside the explicitly Christian realm.

It is in reference to foreign missions that this view has been most clearly developed. Some Roman Catholic missiologists make a sharp distinction between "evangelization" and "conversion." They argue that the injunction to "make disciples of all nations" (Matt. 28:19) commands the worldwide proclamation of the gospel, not the attempt to convert everyone.[7] According to this view the effective presence of authentic Christian witness in every

[7] This paragraph draws particularly on E. Hillman, "The Main Task of Mission," in *Re-Thinking the Church's Mission*, Vol. XIII of *Concilium, op. cit.* (1966), pp. 3–10. It should be noted that such an approach involves a revolution in the attitude towards non-Christian religions. They become the "ordinary" means of salvation, and Christianity the "extraordinary." See H. R. Schlette, *Towards a Theology of Religions* (New York: Herder & Herder, 1966).

country and culture is willed by God as part of the preparation for the Parousia. He uses it as a ferment and leaven to set cultures and societies in motion, to open them up to God's future judgment and redemption. The church's missionary task is to be present everywhere as an eschatological sign, as an explicitly Christian community and a selfless servant of human need. It can leave up to God the question of whether the society as a whole will be Christianized. Christians are not called to feel guilty about the failure to win large numbers of converts or to worry about the decline of Christianity and its minority status in the world. What should concern believers is that the church as sign and witness so often does not authentically point men to Christ, to God's center and God's future for humanity. It may be that it is only when the church is a smaller but more manifestly Christian anticipation of the love and unity of the coming kingdom that it will complete that task of meaningfully preaching and manifesting the gospel to all nations which the Bible tells us is a precondition for final redemption.

Such views, as we have indicated, go much beyond anything in the conciliar documents. They are at most simply made possible by the Council's eschatology and by its abandonment of claims that what is explicitly Christian has a quasi-monopoly of Christ's saving grace. Yet it would be misleading to conclude this section without observing that there is also a positive convergence of liturgy and eschatology in the work of Vatican II.[8]

This convergence is evident from even the most summary statement of the message of the Constitution on the Sacred Liturgy. It understands communal worship as the activity whereby Christian people become active and conscious participants in that redemptive work of God in history which reaches its fullness and completion in Christ's death and resurrection. Involved in this view are parallels to the Reformation's concern for personal faith, a Christocentric focus to all worship, the proclamation of the word, and the priesthood of all believers. As we shall see later in more detail, many of the historic points of controversy between Catholic and Protestant are thus overcome.

---

[8] This convergence is more implicit than explicit, despite the specifically eschatological character of SL 8.

Further, this approach is congruent with an emphasis on the church as the pilgrim people. There is a repudiation of that individualistic piety which has long been just as rampant, in its own way, in Catholic as in Protestant circles. Similarly, there is a rejection of the clericalism which developed when the Mass was turned into an arcane mystery hidden behind rood screens, or—as happened superlatively in the baroque period—into a theatrical spectacle performed by the few for the benefit of the many. Instead, worship is genuinely a function of the whole community. This, in turn, provides ample room for a recognition of the pilgrim state of the church. The ideal of liturgical uniformity is abandoned and replaced by an insistence on the value of diversity and the need for constant adaptation to changing historical and cultural situations. Lastly, the *heilsgeschichtliche* perspective, according to which the liturgies of word and sacrament communicate grace by incorporating believers into salvation history, lends itself easily to a realistically eschatological interpretation in harmony with the "messianic people" motifs of the second chapter of the Constitution on the Church.

To be sure, this is only a possibility. The Constitution on the Liturgy does not itself give an eschatological interpretation, and speaks of worship chiefly as participation in the mystery of redemption and in the body of Christ with little reference to the age to come. Yet once reference to this is made, the difficulty of which we have been speaking is solved. Then the church as the body of Christ is understood not as the kingdom itself but as a sign pointing towards the kingdom. Its worship and sacraments are not the sole or primary means of God's redemptive action, but rather the way men and women become members of that band of witnesses who consciously rejoice in the glorious news of where the universe is heading. Thus liturgy is summit and source, not of the grace-filled life in general but of the Christian testimony to grace. It is central to what God does in and through the church as a distinctive community, but not necessarily central to his redemptive action in individual lives or the world as a whole.

Surely it is only when one speaks with this kind of careful modesty that one can make a persuasive case for the importance of the liturgy. Where going to church is recommended on the grounds that it makes a man a loving person, multitudes will be disillusioned because they have not experienced this. But everyone can see that if the church is to be a community of witnesses it must have at the very heart of its communal life the celebration of the priceless hopes and memories which it exists to proclaim. The early Fathers saw this and said that Christians ought regularly to participate in the liturgy, not necessarily for their own sakes but for the sake of their fellow Christians and the church's testimony in the world. Vatican II implies this through its emphasis on the church as the messianic people which is a sacramental sign, but it fails to make the point clear in its Constitution on the Sacred Liturgy. One could wish it were otherwise. Its answer to the secularist neglect of worship is inadequate.

II

We turn now from the question of *why* the church's mission is to be a worshiping, evangelizing, and explicitly religious and Christian community to the problem of *how* it should be these things. Worship shapes the way Christianity is concretely experienced and actualized. Consequently we confront the issues of sacramentalism versus the living word. We face the question of the sacrifice of the Mass, works-righteousness, merits, grace, the personal-existential nature of faith, the cults of Mary and the saints, relics, and pilgrimages.

From the point of view of traditional Protestant concerns, the basic outline of the Council's treatment of these themes is its most satisfactory accomplishment.[9] It is superior to what is said about the new visions of the world, church, and secular mission. As we

---

[9] The best, though rather technical, discussion of the Constitution on the Liturgy by a Protestant remains that of V. Vajta, "Renewal of Worship," in *Dialogue on the Way, op. cit.,* pp. 101–28. Cf. also E. Schlink, *After the Council* (Philadelphia: Fortress Press, 1968), pp. 50–64; and G. Lindbeck, "Liturgical Reform in the Second Vatican Council," *Lutheran World,* X (1963), 161–71. For a detailed commentary, see J. Jungmann's notes on the text in *Lexikon für Theologie und Kirche. Das Zweite Vatikanische Konzil, op. cit.,* I, 9–109.

have indicated, these are not fully developed and, as we shall see at greater length in the next chapter, are combined with a hierarchism which Protestants question. The new theology of worship, in contrast, pervades the Constitution on the Liturgy thoroughly and consistently; and this theology is not susceptible to Reformation criticisms, at least not in the forms in which they have been traditionally stated. Our exposition will show that objections which Protestants might still have will have to be newly formulated.

It is true that the constitution itself is not as completely acceptable in all its details as is the basic theology of the liturgy which underlies it. Many of the practices which the Reformation regarded as liturgical abuses are not eliminated. We should remember, however, that Vatican II has, by its own account, only begun the task of practical reform and that its fundamental principles point towards vastly greater changes in the future. Further, as members of the liturgical commission which prepared the document have noted,[10] it pays too little attention to the relation between liturgy, personal ethics, and Christian social action. Similarly, it has been pointed out by members of the liturgical commission that there is insufficient stress on the place of the Holy Spirit in worship. A Protestant would like greater emphasis on the connection between "active participation" and living faith. However, these deficiencies could be remedied without difficulty. It also would be easy to eliminate the reminiscences of the cultic language of the past which suggest that God is glorified by liturgical actions rather than by persons and the sanctification of the persons who worship. Lastly, the realistically eschatological dimension is scanted. As we have already mentioned, however, there would be no problem in rewriting the constitution from this perspective because its fundamental outlook is already the *heilsgeschichtliche* one of viewing the liturgy as the celebration of and participation in the *magnalia dei,* the mighty, redemptive acts of God in history.

These points would have to be elaborated in any detailed study

---

[10] Most of the defects in this paragraph are mentioned *inter alia* by G. Diekmann, "The Constitution on the Sacred Liturgy," in *Vatican II: An Interfaith Appraisal, op. cit.,* pp. 17–40.

of the Council's documents. In this study we are limiting our interest to the underlying theology—in this case the theology of the liturgical movement. In the remainder of this chapter, therefore, I shall simply sketch the main features of the understanding of the liturgy which have emerged from this movement, without showing in detail how these are reflected in the Council documents.

There is essential agreement in both the Catholic and non-Catholic liturgical movement on the fundamental objective of this movement. It is to restore the essential pattern or structure of Christian worship as this existed in the early centuries. But it should be restored in a form adapted to the present. In a sense this was also the objective of the sixteenth-century Reformers; but scholarly research has advanced enormously. In contrast to the sixteenth century, there is now considerable agreement among Protestant and Catholic scholars on the eucharistic character of the original pattern and on the implications of this for the renewal of worship. To be sure, the liturgical movement in different denominations varies greatly, but this results not so much from disagreements on basic principles as from the very different context in which these principles are being applied.

In dealing with the liturgical renewal it is still necessary to remind many Protestants that it cannot be identified with ritualism, or aestheticism, or archaism.[11] It is not, in other words, what most low-church Protestants think of as "high church." High-church ritualism was perhaps characteristic of the first phase of the liturgical movement in the nineteenth century of the Anglican Oxford Movement, and of the Roman Catholic Benedictine Movement centering around Solesmes in France which did so much to restore the Gregorian chant. The liturgical movements of the nineteenth century and of the present share a common interest in going back to the sources. However, the source known to the nineteenth-century movement was the High Middle Ages, a ritualistic period concerned with external forms and ceremonies. The present liturgical movement goes back another thousand years; in the

11 For this and the following paragraph, see L. Bouyer, *Liturgical Piety* (Notre Dame, Ind.: Notre Dame University Press, 1955).

process its character and spirit have been transformed. It has gone back to a period of liturgical freedom and diversity, a period when the liturgy was adapted to what were then the contemporary needs. The modern liturgical movement reflects the same qualities. Its spirit is that of taking the earliest liturgical tradition in the Bible and the Fathers as providing not unchanging forms and ceremonies but a normative spirit and principles.

The Roman Catholic liturgical movement seems to have emancipated itself from the early ritualistic phase more completely than has the Protestant liturgical movement. Indeed, it is what most Protestants think of as "low church" rather than "high church." Its concerns are in most cases clearly "evangelical" (in the Reformation, not conversionist-revivalistic, sense of that term). It works for greater simplicity, flexibility, informality, intelligibility, and, above all, active participation on the part of the congregation. This applies to the externals such as responses, prayers, and hymns, but also, and decisively, to the sense of personal-existential involvement. What it wants is the *pro me* of the Reformation and of Pietism, or what the old Methodists would have called "heart experience." To this it adds the insight that the deeply personal experience of God's grace needs the stimulus and control of well-structured and meaningful communal worship in order to be protected from individualistic aberrations and to receive the full dimensions of fellowship with our fellow Christians.

One could also say, to continue using a misleading label, that the liturgical renewal is "low church" in its emphasis on the practical side of Christianity, on the moral transformation of the individual, and on social action. The liturgy, the experience of worship, is inauthentic unless it is correlated with this. One of the most notable features of the Roman Catholic situation is that the liturgical reform group, with few exceptions, is also enthusiastic about social and political reform.

Another preliminary point which needs to be stressed is that the liturgical reform movement in the Roman Catholic Church is only at its beginning. We all know that the Mass is now mostly in the vernacular. The congregations respond more and sing more hymns (including, in some churches, Luther's "A Mighty Fortress

Is Our God"). For the past fifty years Communion has been emphasized more. Opportunities are being provided for eliminating private masses. A greater place is accorded to the sermon. Wherever possible, the altar is moved out from the wall and made into a Communion table with the celebrant standing behind it facing the congregation.

But if the authors of the Constitution on the Liturgy and the present post-conciliar liturgical commission have their way, vastly greater changes are in prospect. The constitution opens up several possibilities. One of these is putting the entire Mass, including the words of consecration, into the vernacular. Another is the substantial revision of the Mass—even its central canon. Other possibilities include giving Communion in both kinds much more frequently than is now authorized, and the gradual disappearance of private masses. To this we must add the possibility of local adaptations to particular needs and traditions so that there would be much greater diversity in forms of worship throughout the world. Thus serious consideration is being given to the use of native music in mission lands—tom-toms in Africa, for example. As a matter of fact, the bishops had experience of this in St. Peter's when Mass was celebrated according to the Ethiopian rite. This may sound bizarre, but it was singularly impressive. Such emphasis on diversity makes it a commonplace in Roman Catholic ecumenical circles to say that if reunion ever comes Anglicans, Congregationalists, Methodists, Presbyterians, and Lutherans might continue worshiping according to their traditional patterns, though these naturally should be revised just as the Roman rite is being revised.

Changes as radical as those we have mentioned will take many decades to reach completion. It will take generations simply to train the priests in the meaning and the spirit of the new liturgy. And then follows the task of training the people. But at the end of thirty to sixty years, a type of worship, a piety, and a religious experience very different from the present one might well be common even among ordinary Roman Catholics. This may sound like a very slow process, but actually it would be phenomenally rapid when one considers how slowly changes are made in the religious realm. In some of the lands in which the Reformation took hold, especially in the Scandinavian countries, it took more than a century for the piety of the people to be much altered. And, as we are all aware, worship in the average Protestant church today differs little from that of a generation ago, despite massive sociological and theological changes. Actually, a new type of Catholic piety is already beginning to emerge. It is particularly powerful in many parishes in France and Germany where the new liturgical movement has been strong for a generation. There many priests and laymen represent a type of spirituality which is profoundly different from the old.

Oddly enough, the conservatives have not resisted these changes as violently as one would expect. In part, this is because the new approaches have not yet been put into practice fully; but in part, it is because the conservatives' emphasis on doctrine and on law makes them think of changes in worship patterns as unimportant.[12] A good many Protestants seem to have a similar view.

III

In order to get at the core of the difference between older and newer views of the sacraments and worship, it is desirable to focus on the theory of sacramental causality.[13] How is it that the sacraments are effective, how do they communicate grace? Obviously, this is only a part of traditional sacramental theology, but for our purposes it is crucial.

Traditional theories reflecting the classical world view can be

---

[12] One Italian commentator at the Council explained the position of the traditionalists by saying that they thought of "liturgy as decorative ceremonial." "The liturgy was considered useful for uncultivated people who need exterior elements to raise themselves to the thought and especially the 'feeling' of spiritual things. To such an extent was it viewed as in some way peripheral to the spiritual life, that practises of individual piety were considered superior to the mass itself." S. Marsili in *Osservatore Romano,* Nov. 4, 1962, p. 2.

[13] For what follows, see especially C. Vagaggini, *Theological Dimensions of the Liturgy* (Collegeville, Minn.: Liturgical Press, 1959). The author of this work is reputed to have played an important part in the drafting of the Constitution on the Liturgy. Cf. also K. Rahner, esp. his "Personal and Sacramental Piety," *Theological Investigations, op. cit.,* II, 109–34; and *The Church and the Sacraments* (Freiburg: Herder & Co., 1963).

divided into two groups: those advocating what was called physical causality and those advocating moral causality. "Physical" in this context does not, of course, mean "material," but rather goes back to the Greek root, *"physis,"* that is, "nature"; but still the physical theories did try to understand sacramental causality as a kind of spiritual analogue of material efficient causality. The sacraments contain grace which is infused into the soul as a spiritual property or attribute. In contrast, the advocates of theories of moral causality could not conceive of grace as being "contained" in the sacraments, and so they said that the performance of the sacramental rite was a moral act which God rewarded by infusing grace into the soul. Some of these theories went so far as to claim that the sacraments constituted a legal title, *titulus iuris,* which set up a kind of claim on God to supply grace.

This brief explanation is obviously unfair. Some of the traditional theologians went to great lengths to protect against abuses of their notions. Still, the fundamental categories of explanation suggested that the sacraments are pipelines channeling grace automatically from the supernatural to the natural level. This gave at least some occasion for the traditional Protestant accusations that the Roman Catholic doctrine was materialistic, mechanical, and magical, and that it substituted salvation by the sacramental works of men for justification by grace through faith.

To this indictment must be added the fact that the traditional theories were individualistic. They pictured saving, forgiving, sanctifying grace as something received into the soul as its property or possession.

In dealing with the newer theology of the liturgy, we shall speak first of its philosophical aspects and then of its theological aspects. On the philosophical side, we shall observe that it substitutes for the traditional theories of sacramental causality the view that the causality of the liturgy, or the sacraments, is symbolic in character. We shall also see that it emphasizes the sacraments as the locus of personal-existential encounter between man and God and that it stresses their character as social rites.

First, liturgy is symbolic action. It is "a system of sensible and intelligible signs." This goes back to the Augustinian definition of the sacraments as "signs of grace which effect or cause the grace which they communicate, the grace which they signify." But now this idea is carried though much more systematically and thoroughly. The sacraments and the liturgy have the kind of causality which symbols have.

In the second place, the sacraments and the liturgy are interpreted in personal-existential terms. For example, what many Catholics consider the best current book on this subject is entitled *Christ: The Sacrament of the Encounter with God*.[14] To speak of personal encounter simply elaborates the notion of symbolic causality, because human beings encounter each other as persons through symbols, that is, through words and gestures which have symbolic import. Symbolic actions can convey more than words by themselves do: for example, walking together, eating together, singing together, a handshake, a kiss. From this point of view, the liturgy, which combines both actions and words, must be considered the most effective means of grace. The actions give vividness and concreteness; but words are also necessary because without them the actions cannot be symbolic in character, for they cannot be understood.

Lastly, we come to sacraments as social rites. Most of us are used to thinking of the social character of a rite as opposed to its personal-existential character. Does not the formal, official, and public necessarily tend towards a diminution of intense personal meaning? Does it not necessarily become routine? Karl Rahner has argued that it does not.[15] He believes that the public and the official is intended to—and sometimes actually does—reinforce or even create intensely personal-existential realities, commitments, and loyalties. This is evident even in the secular domain. A man becomes a citizen of a given country by swearing allegiance, and reinforces this commitment by participating in such rites as saluting the flag, attending political rallies, and voting on election day. These are not only signs of loyalty and commitment to the country, but also signs which cause and effect the loyalty which they signify. They may enable the man later

14 By E. Schillebeeckx (New York: Sheed & Ward, 1963).
15 "Personal and Sacramental Piety," *op. cit.*

willingly to die for his adopted country, something that he might hardly have done had he not become a citizen in this public and official way. The public, official character of a wedding ceremony is also precisely intended not only as a sign of love and fidelity between man and wife but as a reinforcement of that love and fidelity. Without these official formalities, even the most authentically personal, intimate experiences of married love would often find it more difficult to survive the rigors of wedded bliss. These secular analogies, Karl Rahner concludes, tell us much about the nature of the liturgy and of the sacraments. It is precisely because they are public, official symbolic actions of the community that they not only signify but effect or cause the personal-existential reality of union with God and of love and faith. The liturgy can and normally should do this better than private devotions.

We could go on and speak of the relationship between the symbolic view of liturgy and the interpretation of it as a memorial and anticipation of what God has done and will do. It is through this remembering and hoping that God himself and his redemptive acts become present in the liturgical celebration. But this is familiar ground.

We should note that the Roman Catholics who have developed this theory of liturgical and sacramental action do not think of it as in any way compromising the reality of the presence of Christ in the sacrament. This is not a repristination of the view commonly attributed to Zwingli whereby the sacraments are thought of as "mere" signs or symbols. Zwingli's view of signs and symbols was rationalistic. For him, they simply signified a reality quite distinct and different from themselves. In the view of the liturgical movement, symbols and symbolic actions contain a reality which they signify. They effect and cause the reality. Thus Roman Catholic theologians claim that they are in no sense denying that Christ's blood and body are really and substantially present under the species of bread and wine. They are simply explaining the mode of that presence. They are, they say, explaining the way in which the Christ who is really present acts upon the believers. He acts through symbolic causality. We encounter the whole Christ, body and soul together, in the only way in which we can encounter the whole personal reality of another, namely through physical and verbal symbols. As a result of this realism, Roman Catholic theologians consider themselves quite untouched by the papal reaffirmation in *Mysterium fidei* (1965) of transubstantiation and the condemnation of "transignification."[16]

There is a second comment regarding this symbolic-personal-social view of the sacraments. It is the basis for liturgical reforms now taking place. There are two requirements for effective symbolism. First, it must fit the reality which it signifies. In the course of centuries, liturgical changes have made the Mass a poor medium for signifying the reality it contains. It no longer effectively symbolizes union with God in Christ and with one's fellow Christians. For one thing, it has lost the character of a joyful common meal. It must, therefore, be thoroughly revised.

Second, and closely related to this, symbolism and symbolic actions can function effectively as symbols only if there is active and intelligent participation. For this reason we have the contemporary stress on the vernacular and on preaching. In the older physical and moral theories of sacramental causality, it made little difference whether the people understood or not. In the newer view, there must be instruction in the reality signified. This occurs not only through the use of the mother tongue and through religious education but pre-eminently through the proclamation of the word of God or, as the Constitution on the Sacred Liturgy puts it, through the proclamation of the marvelous acts of God. After all, the mighty acts of God are the realities celebrated in the liturgy, and their true character becomes apparent not through didactic instruction but through proclamation, through preaching. Therefore, the liturgy of the word and the sermon are stressed much more than has been traditional in Roman Catholic worship.

We come now to the more specifically theological understanding

[16] Once again, the most thorough Protestant study of this pronouncement is that by V. Vajta, "Eucharistic Faith and Practice in the Encyclical 'Mysterium Fidei,'" *Oecumenica 1966,* ed. W. Kantzenbach and V. Vajta (Minneapolis: Augsburg Publishing House, 1966).

of the character of the liturgy and of the sacraments. How shall we describe the redemptive activity which is symbolized and communicated through them?

In the first place, it is asserted that all God's acts in history from the call of Abraham and the exodus from Egypt to the New Testament period are summed up in Jesus Christ, in his life, death, and resurrection. It is Christ himself who, embracing the whole reality of God's redemptive action, is present and communicates himself in the liturgy. The Christocentricity of this view is quite apparent. It is important to remember this because it means that extra-liturgical practices which do not focus on Christ are pushed to the periphery.

In the second place, it should be observed that God's redemptive activity is understood as having three aspects. First, there is his initiative, that is, his address to man; second, there is man's response; and third, there is God's transformation of man. All three of these aspects come from God. Indeed, it is Christ who is perfectly all three. He is the perfect Word, the perfect revelation of God, but he is also the perfect man, the perfect worshiper of God, the perfect adorer. As perfect creature, perfect adorer of the Father, he is also perfectly obedient, that is, the perfect sacrifice. Lastly, Christ is the one whom God has raised from the dead; he is the firstfruits of the kingdom, of the new humanity, of the new creation.

Worship, therefore, is Christ's own worship of the Father. The liturgical action is Christ's action. He is at every point the agent, the one who acts and takes the initiative. The key to understanding our part in the liturgy are the two words "participation" and "incorporation." To participate in the liturgy is to participate in Christ's worship; it is for him to incorporate us into himself, to make us part of himself, part of his body.

IV

It will be observed that in the context of this understanding of the liturgy there is no longer room for the central traditional

Protestant accusation that Catholics teach justification in part by works and by merit. Everything is embraced in Christ's actions, in the *sola gratia*. As a result, to take just two examples, the Catholic affirmation of the *ex opere operato* (i.e., sacramental actions are efficacious simply through being done) and the sacrifice of the Mass are reinterpreted. The *ex opere operato* is made to refer to the divine initiative, not to the idea that the sacrament is effective even without living faith.[17] In order to make this point intelligible we can refer once again to our secular analogy. A man becomes a citizen entirely through the action of the state; the swearing-in ceremony is effective simply by being rightly performed, but to be a citizen really willing, for example, to die for one's country, one must make a personal response, one must actively participate in the ceremony.

Similarly, in reference to the sacrifice of the Mass, this is now more clearly understood, not as our meritorious action, but as Christ's own sacrifice of himself. The church offers Christ only by reason of the fact that he incorporates the church into his self-offering. Only because of this can one say that the worshipers, congregation, and priest together offer the Divine Victim. They do this only in the sense that Christ joins believers to his sacrifice so closely that what he does and what they do cannot be meaningfully distinguished.[18]

---

[17] Rahner, "Personal and Sacramental Piety," *op. cit.,* p. 124.

[18] The possibilities of *rapprochement* in this area of traditionally bitter controversy are well illustrated by the statement prepared in 1967 by the Roman Catholic and Lutheran participants in conversations sponsored by the American Bishops' Conference and the United States Committee for the Lutheran World Federation. One paragraph reads as follows: "Further, the Catholic affirmation that the church 'offers Christ' in the mass has in the course of the last half century been increasingly explained in terms which answer Lutheran fears that this detracts from the full sufficiency of Christ's sacrifice. The members of the body of Christ are united through Christ with God and with one another in such a way that they become participants in his worship, his self-offering, his sacrifice to the Father. Through this union between Christ and Christians, the eucharistic assembly 'offers Christ' by consenting in the power of the Holy Spirit to be offered by him to the Father. Apart from Christ we have no gifts, no worship, no sacrifice of our own to offer to God. All we can plead is Christ, the sacrificial lamb and victim whom the Father himself has given us." The attached footnote cites similar statements regarding the sacrificial nature of the Eucharist from Luther's "A Treatise on the New Testament," in *Luther's Works* (Philadelphia: Fortress Press, 1961), XXXV, 98–101; from Vatican II's *Presbyterorum ministerio* 2; and from Karl Rahner's "Die vielen Messen und

These are simply examples of the way in which the new under-standing of the liturgy overcomes traditional Protestant objections to Catholic positions. But it should not be supposed that what we have here is simply an adoption of a Reformation or Protestant position. The contemporary liturgical renewal goes beyond what Protestants have traditionally held.

It asserts, in the first place, that Christian experience is essen-tially communal, not individualistic. The Catholics, in their own way, have been just as individualistic as Protestants. One belonged to the church and went to Mass in order to receive grace for one's benefit, for the sake of saving one's own soul. Now, however, the emphasis has shifted to viewing worship as a matter not simply of our own individual relations to God but of incorporation into Christ through and together with our neighbors.

In the second place, this understanding of the liturgy and of Christian experience does not concentrate one-sidedly on the cross and forgiveness of sin. To be sure, forgiveness is an essential part of Christian experience. But it is not the whole nor even necessarily the most important part. Christian experience is fundamentally a matter of reconciliation, of being joined to Christ, not only in his death, but also in his life and resurrection. This is the idea which is expressed when it is said that the liturgy, the Mass, should be looked at as an Easter event.

In the third place, there is in the current phases of the liturgical movement an increasingly strong eschatological emphasis. The liturgy and the sacraments incorporate us into the new humanity, the new creation, for in becoming joined to Christ we become joined to him who is the beginning of the kingdom of God. The liturgical action is a foretaste of the coming kingdom; the Lord's Supper is an anticipation of the heavenly feast.

It must be admitted that at each of these three points the Re-formation—in part contrary to the intentions of the Reformer— failed to get rid of medieval distortions. At each of these points traditional Catholic and Protestant worship have both been de-

das eine Opfer," *Zeitschrift für katholische Theologie,* LXXI (1949), 267, 288. See *Lutherans and Catholics in Dialogue III: The Eucharist as Sacrifice* (ob-tainable from the U.S.A. National Committee for the Lutheran World Federa-tion and the Publications Office, United States Catholic Conference), pp. 189–90.

ficient. They have both tried, although in different ways, to perpetuate in the modern world a medieval pattern of guilt-ridden preoccupation with one's own salvation. It may be that these deficiencies have largely contributed to the increasing irrelevance of Christianity in our world.

Before leaving this topic, we should make a reservation. It is, after all, not the theology of worship which is decisive but rather practice. Catholic worship is only now beginning to be reformed along the lines proposed by the liturgical movement. On the level of practice, there are many patterns which have been so sanctified by tradition, or even dogmatized, that they are now practically impossible to eliminate, even though they are not in harmony with the theology of the liturgy. Private masses, the adoration of the sacrament, and many other extra-liturgical devotions are examples of this. The Roman Catholic Church is so thoroughly committed to these that it can at most discourage them; it cannot eliminate them without repudiating past dogmatic decisions. Apparently the most we can hope for is that they will become less and less important in the actual practice of Catholics in the future. If this happens to a major degree along the lines indicated by the Council, much Catholic worship and spirituality would become notably better than anything now existing on a large scale in Protestant denominations.

In conclusion, however, we must return to the secularist's problem. For him, the question is not whether the liturgical movement is compatible with the Bible and the Reformation, but whether it has any chance of success in the modern world. Our age, after all, is one which is highly individualistic, has no deep sense of community, and, furthermore, is literalistic, with little responsiveness to symbols. The kind of religious experience which is nourished and formed by the liturgy, however authentically Christian it may be, seems doomed in such an environment.

These observations are more apropos when applied to Protestants than to Catholics. The habits of the Catholic people give the liturgical movement more to work with, more substance to transform, and therefore greater chance of success. The conviction that the Mass, that communal worship, is important has been maintained despite grave distortions. There is, further, the tradition of placing great emphasis on Christ's real presence.[19] The problem of renewal is simply that of enlarging this sense of sacramental reality to include Christ's presence throughout the whole liturgy, in the preaching of the gospel as well as in the sacrament, and of leading the people to think of this as an active presence, in which they participate, not simply an inert one which they adore. The problem in Protestantism is more serious, for here the liturgical substance has been largely evacuated, and it seems to be much more difficult to reintroduce what has been lost than to reshape what is still present.

But is it really possible for even a reformed Catholic liturgical piety long to resist the acids of modernity? My own impressions are that the answer to this question largely depends not on empirical data but on theological and philosophical considerations. What kind of being is man? Is he inevitably and ineradicably a creature who needs communal rituals and symbolic actions to express and effect that basic consensus which every society needs for its survival? Does he, as a social creature, need declarations of allegiance and salutes to the flag on the secular level, and something comparable on the religious one? If he does, then when one set of religious or political rituals loses its power another set will replace it. These rituals may not be Christian: they may perhaps be the rituals of chauvinistic nationalism, communism, nazism, or some other secular faith. At any rate, if this is the way human beings are, then a reformed and restored pattern of worship which authentically reflects the gospel of reconciliation better than our present patterns may in the long run be the only way through which the Christian faith will remain active and living in the world.

This is a matter on which disputes will long continue in the

---

[19] "Today, however, when Lutheran theologians read contemporary Catholic expositions, it becomes clear to them that the dogma of transubstantiation intends to affirm the fact of Christ's presence and of the change which takes place, and is not an attempt to explain how Christ becomes present. When the dogma is understood in this way, Lutherans find that they also must acknowledge that it is a legitimate way of attempting to express the mystery, even though they continue to believe that the conceptuality associated with transubstantiation is misleading and therefore prefer to avoid the term." *Lutherans and Catholics in Dialogue III,* p. 196.

Protestant realm, but the Catholic is doctrinally committed. After Vatican II, he cannot deny the importance of the eucharistic worship of the community, joining together the liturgies of both word and sacrament. *Diakonia* and *koinonia* are also essential, but from one perspective at least "the liturgy is the summit toward which the activity of the Church is directed at the same time that it is the fountain from which all her power flows" (SL 10).

4

ECUMENISM AND ECCLESIASTICAL STRUCTURES

We turn now from the church's secular service of the world and its religious activities to its *koinonia,* its character as a community of unifying love. The major changes in this area are in the understanding of the structures and authority of the church and in ecumenical attitudes. *Koinonia* is first of all a matter of interpersonal fellowship, but it also finds expression and is preserved and fostered by the structures of the community. Ecclesiastical structures, it is true, can also be looked at from the point of view of their relation to *diakonia* and *leitourgia,* as means of organizing and maintaining service, worship, and proclamation. The Council often adopts these perspectives, but its main concern in dealing with the institutional side of the church's life is with *koinonia,* with the promotion of the universal, catholic, ecumenical love, freedom, and faithfulness which should characterize the people of God.

The manifestation of *koinonia,* as the making visible of the internal unity of believers in the Spirit, is central to the missionary task if, as the Council proposes, the purpose of the church is to serve as an efficacious sign of God's reconciling and unifying redemption. Most Protestants seem to agree, for they think that the Roman Catholic Church's institutional and theological distortions of *koinonia* are the greatest continuing hindrances to Christian unity and to the Christian authenticity of that church's mission.

From now on, then, we shall be dealing with the most obstinate barriers between the churches. The center of the debate in our day has shifted away from the issues connected with the material principle of the Reformation, away from the doctrine of justification. New views of world and church, of *diakonia* and *leitourgia* as we have sketched them, escape from the classical Protestant objections, at least as traditionally formulated. These views do not exalt the creature at the expense of the Creator, nor do they imperil the sovereignty of grace and the all-sufficiency of faith. The kingdom of God is a gift and promise, not an individual or collective achievement within history. The church is the pilgrim people and the selfless servant of mankind. Her worship is a matter of personal encounter in living faith with God through Christ.

However, the problem of the church's authority versus the formal principle of the Reformation, the *sola scriptura,* still remains. Two major Roman claims, however profoundly they may be modified in the context of the new outlook, still exalt the ecclesiastical institution at the expense of the authority which the Protestant believes must be assigned to Scripture. The first is that the Roman church alone is institutionally "perfect" or complete, that all the basic elements of its hierarchical structure, including the papacy, have been divinely instituted. This goes beyond any clear word of Scripture. Related to this is a second claim that this church is infallible in the sense that God sees to it that it cannot err when it officially declares a doctrine to be *de fide.*

The two claims depend on each other. The Roman Catholic asserts the institutional, structural completeness of his church, not as directly certified by Scripture but on the basis of a supposedly infallible interpretation of revelation. And he affirms that the Roman Church has the competence to interpret revelation infallibly because it alone is endowed with the institutional completeness which God has willed.

Further, all other apparently irresolvable issues depend on magisterial infallibility. Purgatory and the cult of the saints and Mary, for example, can conceivably be reformed and reinterpreted, as some Roman Catholics are now attempting to do, so that they do not conflict with the Bible. They might become, so to speak, legitimate theological opinions and acceptable optional pious practices. But for anyone who accepts the *sola scriptura,* the church does not have the authority to make them more than this.[1] To define them as dogmas *de fide* is to go beyond what faithfulness to Scripture demands. To the Protestant it seems in fact—even if this is repudiated by Roman Catholic theory—to add to the public revelation and thus imperil the sole lordship of the Christ to whom the Bible witnesses. (In this sense, it should be observed, the *sola scriptura* derives from the same source as the *sola fide,* for both are intended to assert as unequivocally as possible that Christ is Lord.[2])

Previously we have noted the way in which a realistically eschatological perspective increases the missionary urgency of Christian unity. In this chapter we shall try to show that, to a degree barely hinted at by Vatican II, this perspective makes possible the lowering of the hierarchical barriers. The papacy alone remains as an apparently irreducible obstacle, and even here, we shall suggest, the ultimate issue is the one discussed in the final chapter of this study—dogmatic infallibility versus the *sola scriptura.*

I

In the classical framework, where the mission of the church is thought of as primarily that of proclaiming or mediating grace to individuals, there is no absolutely compelling reason for Christians to be visibly united in order to carry out their task. This is particularly true on the Protestant side. But traditionally for Catholics also, it is not so much that the church (meaning in this context the

---

[1] For a more detailed exposition of the argument of this paragraph see G. Lindbeck, "Reform and Infallibility," *Cross Currents,* XI (1961), 345–56; and "The Problem of Doctrinal Development and Contemporary Protestant Theology," in *Man as Man and Believer,* Vol. XXI of *Concilium, op. cit.* (1967), pp. 133–49.

[2] Most contemporary Protestant dogmaticians who profess to stand in the Reformation tradition think of this as the crucial issue in the *sola scriptura* controversy. See, e.g., the essays by G. Ebeling and K. E. Skydsgaard in *Schrift und Tradition,* ed. K. E. Skydsgaard and L. Vischer (Zurich, 1963); and Karl Barth, *Kirchliche Dogmatik* (Zurich, 1932), Vol. I, pt. 2, p. 641.

"Roman Church") will fulfill its purpose in some qualitatively better sense if divisions are overcome as that more people will benefit from its services. Union is important even in the context of the individualistically conceived mission of the church because it is painful for Christian brethren to be separated at the Lord's table, and because of the positive command of Christ. Nevertheless, the reason that visible unity is urgently necessary for mission is not clear. It is not built into the very concept of the church.

In a realistically eschatological framework, in contrast, the church's job is to be the sign among the nations of "God's eschatologically triumphant mercy" (as Karl Rahner expresses it).[3] The church is to show that grace is precisely the reconciliation and the unification of all things in Christ. It thus becomes obvious that Christians must be reconciled among themselves and also must be reconcilers in the world if they are to be credible and persuasive witnesses; if their witness is to prepare the world for that reconciliation which is in Christ, they must remind men of the true shape of the future which God wills for humanity. The ecumenical endeavor to manifest visibly the unity of all Christians is fundamental to the church's nature as sign and instrument of the eschatological unity of the divided world. This last sentence paraphrases the programmatic introduction to the Constitution on the Church (art. 1). It is really the basic charter of Roman Catholic ecumenism. By it the Roman Catholic Church is now doctrinally committed to the urgency of the ecumenical enterprise more thoroughly than is any other church.[4]

The energies which have previously been thrown into the campaign to get other Christians to "return to Rome" are now solemnly—doctrinally—being directed towards the work of ecumeni-

---

[3] *The Church and the Sacraments, op. cit.,* p. 14.

[4] The Roman Church thinks of itself as "catholic" *par excellence.* Consequently, when it recognizes, as has now been done, that "divisions among Christians prevent the Church from effecting the fullness of catholicity proper to her" making it "more difficult to express in actual life her full catholicity in all its aspects" (E 4), then the ecumenical task becomes doctrinally even more urgent for her than for other churches. The Decree on Ecumenism, in harmony with this, says that ecumenism is a chief concern of the Council (art. 1), pertaining to everyone (art. 5) and to all dimensions of the church's life (art. 6). For a summary documentation of the immense importance of ecumenism for Vatican II see J. Feiner's commentary on the decree, *Lexikon für Theologie und Kirche. Das Zweite Vatikanische Konzil, op. cit.,* II, 41.

cal reconciliation. The difference is immense. It is a serious mistake for Protestants to argue, as they sometimes do, that there has been no real change because the ultimate objective still remains "return."[5] That is, since Rome does not recognize the possibility of giving up any of its dogmas, any reunion must take place on Roman terms. This is in part true, even though, as we shall see, the conditions are not as rigidly predetermined as Protestants (and many Catholics) generally suppose. Yet a fundamental change has taken place. Preliminary steps, as the Decree on Ecumenism makes clear, are important in and of themselves even if they do not lead to full church unity.[6] Within the new perspective, everything which authentically promotes communication and cooperation, common worship and witness, is to be treasured as increasing the missionary sign value of Christian unity. This is obviously antithetical to the old approach which assiduously avoided preliminary and partial manifestations of unity on the grounds that these made it less apparent that Rome alone is the one true church and therefore diminished the urgency of the call to return.[7]

From this older rigid point of view, it will be recalled, the churches closest to Rome could be considered the most dangerous, and Anglican orders, for example, were bewailed by some as a particularly delusive mimicry of the genuine ecclesiological article.[8]

[5] Any explicit reference to "return" was assiduously avoided by the Council. The progressives often argue that all the churches entering into a reunited church should become so thoroughly renewed that it is more appropriate to speak of them as "seeking to converge towards a point which is certainly beyond their present positions." Y. Congar, "L'originalité de l'entreprise oecumenique," in *Chrétiens en dialogue* (Paris: Cerf, 1964), p. 116. Nevertheless, however many objectionable elements may be removed, the notion of "return" continues to have validity as long as Rome claims (as it must in order to retain its self-identity) to be, and to have always been, in some sense the one true church.

[6] "Before the whole world, let all Christians profess their faith. . . . Cooperation among all Christians vividly expresses that bond which already unites them, and it sets in clearer relief the features of Christ" (E 12). For common worship, cf. E 8; cooperation on Bible translations, DR 22; in the mission field, CMA 15, 41; among laymen, AL 27; and in reference to the church in the modern world, CMW 88, 90.

[7] For an expression of this attitude, see E. F. Hanahoe, *Catholic Ecumenism* (Washington, D.C.: Catholic University Press, 1953). For the history of Roman Catholic concern with Christian unity, see G. Tavard, *Two Centuries of Ecumenism* (Notre Dame, Ind.: Fides Press, 1960).

[8] J. J. Hughes, "The Papal Condemnation of Anglican Orders," *Journal of Ecumenical Studies*, IV (1967), 235–67, esp. p. 237 where Cardinal Vaughan, archbishop of Westminster, is cited as holding this opinion.

Further, movements towards unity apart from Rome, such as ecumenism in its early phases, were sometimes viewed as diabolical. Now these attitudes have been reversed. The Council describes the ecumenical movement, even in its non–Roman Catholic development, as the work of the Holy Spirit (E 1). Those who think in the newer terms rejoice at all reconciliation between Christians, even when it occurs among non-Catholics. Such Catholics delight in all renewal, whether on the Roman or non-Roman side, which diminishes disagreements even when there is no evidence that it will contribute to "return" in the foreseeable future.

Another change is that the program of "return" tended to identify unity with uniformity in a way that is nothing short of detestable to contemporary Roman Catholic ecumenists. Diversity within the church is necessary because a church which is homogeneous, which does not reconcile groups of different races, cultures, classes, liturgies, spiritualities, church structures, and even theologies, is not an effective sign or agent of reconciliation. This point is clearly stated, even if not with all the consequences, in the Constitution on the Church and the Decree on Ecumenism.[9] Diversity, the Council says, is inseparable from catholicity.

Nevertheless, full organizational unity remains an unquestionable good and the unquestionable goal for even *avant garde* Roman Catholic theologians.[10] Authentic witness cannot be opposed to institutionalism, for God has created the kind of world in which belief-systems must be institutionalized if they are to be effective. Without institutions, without embodiment in an organized society, the witness to Christ would disappear, or at least would not be an efficacious agent, a leaven within history working by both con-

[9] E 4, 16, 17; C 5 ff., 12 ff., 20 ff. Cf. SL 37–39, 65, 77, 107, 110, 119, 123.
[10] The concrete shape of this "organizational unity" is in many respects left undefined. For example it is said that the "rights and privileges" of the Eastern patriarchates "should be re-established in accord with the ancient traditions of each Church. . . . The rights and privileges in question are those which flourished when East and West were in union, though they should be somewhat adapted to modern conditions" (EC 9). Feiner comments on the parallel passage, E 16, that this "has universal ecumenical importance." A union of divided churches "can only be thought of as a union of different 'types of churches' which preserve their particularity and 'canonical' autonomy within the unity willed by Christ" (*op. cit.* [p. 104, n. 4]). Clearly the organizational pattern within which these objectives could be realized would be vastly different from that of contemporary Roman Catholicism.

tradiction and contribution to prepare mankind for the kingdom. Clearly the institutional church must be visibly united if it is to be an effective sign of God's unity and peace. A divided church contradicts in its organizational forms what it testifies to in its words. It is claimed that the testimony of what the church is, the testimony of its visible structures, is more powerful than the gospel which it proclaims simply with its lips. For these reasons the necessity of an institutionally united church is maintained just as vigorously by those whose imaginations have been captured by the new vision as it is by conservatives, even though their reasons are substantially different.

This brings us to the claim that the Roman Catholic Church is the one true church, a claim which, as we have mentioned, makes many Protestants think genuine ecumenical dialogue with Rome is impossible. This may have been true in the traditional interpretation. According to this interpretation all other Christian communions, with the partial exception of the ancient Orthodox bodies of the East, are not really churches at all; they are, rather, false and perverted semblances of the genuine article. Now, however, the claim to be the one true church tends more and more to be limited to the single point that the Roman Catholic communion alone has *all* the institutional elements willed by Christ for his church. Other churches have many of these elements: the Bible, preaching, the liturgy and some or all of the sacraments, a regular ministry, in some cases even bishops. They also have the Holy Spirit and his gifts of faith, hope, and love, as well as the social and moral fruits which spring from these.[11] Indeed, at all these points it is possible that at some times and places they may be superior to Roman Catholicism, and that, as the Council itself has acknowledged, Catholics can learn from them.[12] But, so the argument goes, Christ also willed the Petrine, the papal, office to serve as the institutional agent of unity for the universal church, and this divinely willed office is precisely what Rome alone has

[11] This point is made in E 4 and developed at length in E 14–23 in reference to both the Orthodox and Protestant churches.

[12] "Nor should we forget that whatever is wrought by the grace of the Holy Spirit in the hearts of our separated brethren can contribute to our own edification" (E 4).

among the churches. Thus it is in the sense of institutional completeness or "perfection" that Rome is the one true church, not in the sense that other Christian bodies do not have many elements of the church or are in no sense churches. The Constitution on the Church does not say that the church *is* the Roman Catholic Church, but that it *subsists* in it (C 8). This provides the basis for those recommendations for ecumenical dialogue and cooperation which are developed in the Decree on Ecumenism (chap. 2) but which it is not our business to examine in this consideration of theological principles.

Enough has been said about those principles to make evident how overwhelmingly urgent ecumenism is in the new perspective. To the degree that this outlook becomes pervasive, the Roman Catholic Church will adopt the policy of doing nothing separately which can be done equally well or better in cooperation with other churches. The establishment of joint parishes, of which we have seen recent experimental examples,[13] becomes theologically mandatory in some situations. The logic of this position, as indicated by certain recent Roman Catholic discussions, even opens up the possibility of limited intercommunion under certain circumstances, not only with separated Orthodox churches, but with separated Protestant ones.[14] Already under the impulsion of this type of ecumenical thinking, the Roman communion has in five years become more active in dialogue and cooperation than have some other denominations which have been involved in the organized ecumenical movement since its inception fifty years ago.

This has resulted not only from theological changes but also from practical developments which are persuading many Roman ecclesiasts that their church has less to lose and more to gain even institutionally from ecumenical activities than was true in the past. Nevertheless, doctrine is so important for Roman Catholic-

[13] In Kansas City and Chicago.
[14] A succinct statement of this position is G. Baum, "Communicatio in Sacris," *The Ecumenist*, II (1964), 60–62. For what is perhaps the most solid available investigation of the validity of Protestant Eucharists from a Catholic point of view, see F. J. van Beeck, "Towards an Ecumenical Understanding of the Sacraments," *Journal of Ecumenical Studies*, III (1966), 57–112. This, of course, goes beyond the Council which denies the "genuine and total reality" of Protestant Eucharists but without specifying exactly what is lacking (E 22).

ism that these prudential considerations would not have received concrete implementation if the Council had not begun officially to ratify the theological developments which we have described.

II

In order to grasp the possible future significance of Roman Catholic ecumenism, we must now turn to a consideration of its limits. In this chapter we are particularly concerned with the limits imposed by ecclesiastical structures. It is not enough simply to recall the traditional understanding of the divisive dogmas regarding priests, bishops, and popes, because these are now being interpreted very differently within the new framework. They can be given an operational meaning which is in most respects thoroughly evangelical from the Reformation point of view. To be sure, the full practical realization of this new understanding would require what now seem to us unimaginably great structural transformations. But these transformations are becoming theologically, even if not yet practically, conceivable. So we must sketch them if we are to isolate the apparently irreducible core of doctrinal disagreement.

The operational significance of Roman teachings regarding priesthood, episcopacy, and papacy changes radically once these are removed from the framework supplied by the classical picture of the church. Seen within this framework, the church is an institutional, hierarchical pyramid towering up towards heaven in which all power, all authority, and (in popular imagination, if not scholastic theory) all grace flows downward from the papal apex through the successive levels of bishops and priests to the wholly passive and submissive laity. Here the church is the institution; ordinary believers, even when they gather together for mutual edification, do not constitute the church, but are rather its clientele.

In contrast, there is the emerging vision of the messianic pilgrim people which gains its communal identity through worship. Where this concept is taken seriously, it is above all the laity, the *laos,* which is the church. The clergy, whether of high or low degree, are viewed as servants of the servants of God. This, of course, is a traditional formula, but now the attempt is being made to give it effective meaning. The hierarchy is not so much the source and center of the church as its minister, which exists in order to equip and aid the people in their service, witness, and worship. The hierarchy is instrumental rather than constitutive, for the people can continue to exist, even if miserably and with difficulty, when its leaders fail and its institutional structures falter. The chief emphasis falls not on monarchical authority but on consensus and cooperation. To put it technically, the theory of the church becomes, as the Council declared, collegial.

This shift of outlook is present in the Council documents, but only obscurely and partially, even in the doctrinally basic third chapter of the Constitution on the Church, where the doctrine of episcopal collegiality is expounded.[15]

As we know, there were those who feared that papal primacy would be endangered by any emphasis on the bishops. These people were tenacious in resisting such an emphasis, and everything possible was done to reassure them. This was accomplished so successfully that the non-Catholic reader can easily be deceived into supposing that nothing has changed. He is all too likely to remember chiefly that "the college or body of bishops has no authority unless it is understood together with the Roman Pontiff. . . . His power of primacy over all, both pastors and faithful, remains whole and intact" (C 22), and his suspicions of *immobilisme* will in all probability be reinforced by the notoriously ambiguous *nota explicativa praevia*.[16]

By itself, chapter three seems to come straight out of a static, two-story world view. Without actually asserting this, it seems to say that the episcopacy and the papacy were established by Christ

[15] The Council, to be sure, speaks explicitly of the collegiality only of the hierarchy, but a number of theologians have remarked that a deepening of the notion involves also its application to the relation of hierarchy and laity. See C. Moeller and Y. Congar in *Vatican II: An Interfaith Appraisal, op. cit.,* p. 133 and p. 248 respectively; and J. Ratzinger, "The Pastoral Implications of Episcopal Collegiality," in *The Church and Mankind, op. cit.,* pp. 39–67.

[16] For commentary and literature on this *Nota* (which is attached to all the texts of the Constitution on the Church) see G. Philips and J. Ratzinger in *Lexikon für Theologie und Kirche. Das Zweite Vatikanische Konzil,* I, 155, and 350–59, respectively.

in virtually their present form when he was here on earth. Further, Peter and the other apostles seem to have a certain logical and temporal priority to the rest of the church (C 19). The results are twofold. First, the principle of collegiality seems to be restricted—though this, fortunately, is not actually stated—to the bishops alone. Second, the church as the body of Christ and the people of God is somehow secondary, a product of the ecclesiastical institution. It is easy to see from this why one Greek Orthodox commentator has expressed the fear that the Constitution on the Church has simply compounded the mistake of the First Vatican Council. He suggests that it raises the episcopacy to the level of the pope, rather than reintegrating the whole hierarchy, bishops and pope together, into the people of God.[17]

However, a different picture emerges when one makes not this chapter but the first two chapters the systematic center of the constitution. If one focuses on the church as the people of God in which, as the fourth chapter on the laity suggests, even the lowliest member has the right and the responsibility to make his voice heard (C 39), then it becomes natural to think of the entire company of Christians, and not simply the hierarchy, as collegially structured. As Bishop Edelby suggested in Rome, Christ first calls "believers to whom the preaching of the gospel rightly belongs, then gives them apostles, and finally chooses a head of the apostolic college so that this college will remain united."[18] When understood in these terms, the relation of collegiality, which the Council has declared to exist between bishops and pope, extends by analogy to the relation between bishops, priests, and deacons, and also to that between the laity and their pastors.

The Council permits, although it by no means demands, such an interpretation of collegiality in terms of the concept of the people of God. If one follows this line, then present organizational forms should be profoundly modified at every level. There should be a far greater degree of active participation and initiative by all mem-

---

[17] "It is an attempt to complete but not correct the formula of Vatican II by extending the idea of divine right by analogy also to the bishops." Nikos Nissiotis, "The Main Ecclesiological Problems of Vatican II," *Journal of Ecumenical Studies,* II (1965), 35.

[18] *Informations catholiques internationales,* Nov. 15, 1963, p. 14.

bers of the church in the processes of decision-making and their implementation. This applies even in the area of doctrine. Structures should be created which make the formation and expression of the *sensus fidelium* effective. Lay participation in government is desirable, not only in the election of members of the hierarchy as was done in the early church, but directly as regular delegates to regional and ecumenical councils.

Technically this is not "democracy" because the hierarchy would retain what might be called a veto power and because it could, if necessary, act without the consent of the governed. But such measures would be considered unfortunate and the attempt would be made to order the church in such a way as to keep them at a minimum. The church is essentially a community of love and freedom and it must maximize consensus and freedom, that is, collegiality, by the very way in which it is structured.[19]

III

This brings us to the question of what happens to the traditional dogmatic stress on the hierarchy when it is viewed within the context of this new interpretive framework, this new vision of the church. I shall simply indicate with the utmost brevity why I think the ecumenical problems connected with the priesthood and episcopacy may be resolvable, and then turn to a somewhat more extended comment on the papacy. There is at least some hope for agreement between Catholic and Protestant on the priesthood, that is, the ministry of the word and sacraments.[20] This is true because, first, there is fundamental agreement on the divinely ordained (*de iure divino*) character of this office. The Reformers also insisted that it is given to the church by God. The minister is not simply the representative of the people (though he is also that), nor is every Christian authorized by his baptism to exercise

[19] The most comprehensive progressive treatment of this subject is by Hans Küng, *Structures of the Church* (New York: Thomas Nelson & Sons, 1964).

[20] The argument of this paragraph is more fully developed in my article "Karl Rahner and a Protestant View of the Sacramentality of the Ministry," *Proceedings of the Catholic Theological Society of America*, XXI (1966), 262–88; reprinted in *Oecumenica 1967, op. cit.*, pp. 282–301.

the functions of the official, public proclamation of the word and the administration of the sacraments. The disagreement has been on another question, that of the sacramental character of the priesthood as an inherent *habitus* or power imprinted on the soul which is an indispensable condition (most particularly) for performing the eucharistic sacrifice. However, some Roman Catholics are now arguing that this view of the priesthood is a matter not of dogma but of theological theory. They argue that it is possible to understand the ministerial, sacramental character of ordination (as the Lutheran confessional writings suggest would be acceptable)[21] in terms of the personal-existential (not ontological-institutional) gifts of the Spirit promised in view primarily of the proclamation of the word rather than the administration of the sacraments. Further, new views of validity are being developed which do not depend on mechanical, "pipeline" theories of the transmission of hierarchical powers and which make it possible to envisage exceptional circumstances under which even the Eucharist can be celebrated legitimately by those who are not regularly ordained. The Reformers and a great many of their heirs would find these proposals satisfactory, even though they would, of course, like to see them officially approved by the Roman Church. There is no hint of such approval as yet.

Once these points are granted, the way is open for agreement on the episcopacy also. The Lutheran confessions express a "deep desire to maintain" the historic episcopacy "provided that the bishops stop raging against our churches."[22] The Reformers viewed the establishment of separate orders as an emergency measure which they hoped would be temporary.[23] To be sure, they also contended that there are no grounds for saying that the distinction

---

[21] Apology of the Augsburg Confession, art. XIII, sec. 7 in *The Book of Concord*, ed. and trans. T. G. Tappert (Philadelphia: Muhlenberg Press, 1959), p. 212.

[22] Apology of the Augsburg Confession, art. XIV, in *ibid.,* pp. 214, 215. Cf. Smalcald Articles, X, in *ibid.,* p. 314.

[23] The fullest summary and discussion available in English of the relevant research on the position of the Reformers is in Küng, *Structures of the Church, op. cit.,* pp. 106-48. He argues for the acceptability by Rome of a Lutheran "episcopalianism" such as that of E. Schlink, "Apostolic Succession," *The Coming Christ and the Coming Church* (Philadelphia: Fortress Press, 1968), pp. 186-233.

within the ministerial office between priests or ministers and bishops is divinely ordained. Supervisory functions are involved in the ministry of word and sacraments, and the assignment of special responsibility for these to a particular group of ministers, to the bishops, is a matter of human, not divine, ordinance. However, the Roman Catholics are not officially committed on this crucial point and so could conceivably adopt a similar position. It is true that the Constitution on the Church asserts that "by episcopal consecration is conferred the fullness of the sacrament of orders" (art. 21). But this statement does not specify whether the "fullness" refers to the "essence" or the "exercise" of the ministry. Consequently, it leaves open the possibility that the differentiation between priest and bishop is a matter of human, not divine, law,[24] rare though this opinion is in contemporary Catholic thought.

However, when we turn to the papacy these theoretical possibilities of concord seem to disappear. To be sure, *rapprochement* on the practical level is conceivable. The new perspectives favor reforming the papal office so that it would lose its unilaterally authoritarian features and become an institutional means not of monarchically ruling but of collegially preserving the visible unity of the universal church. This would make it operationally acceptable, not only to the sixteenth-century Protestant signers of the Appendix to the Smalcald articles,[25] but also to many of their successors. Yet the vital objection would remain that, for Roman Catholics, it is a matter of divine law, not simply historical development, that this center of unity should be the Petrine See.

Before proceeding, we must observe in more detail what is meant by the statement that the papal office might become "operationally acceptable," for otherwise we shall misconstrue the nature of the doctrinal disagreement. At first glance it might seem im-

[24] B. Dupuy reaches the same conclusion by means of a somewhat different argument in "Is There a Dogmatic Distinction Between the Function of Priests and the Function of Bishops?" in *Apostolic Succession*, Vol. XXXIV of *Concilium, op. cit.* (1968), pp. 74–86.

[25] They agreed concerning the pope that "if he would allow the Gospel, we, too, may concede to him that superiority over the bishops which he possesses by human right, making this concession for the sake of peace and general unity among the Christians who are now under him and who may be in the future." *Book of Concord, op. cit.*, pp. 316–17.

possible that the papacy could be deprived of its objectionable monarchical features. We recall that the First Vatican Council, nearly a hundred years ago, proclaimed that the pope has ordinary, supreme, and immediate jurisdiction over the universal church and that his *ex cathedra* pronouncements are valid "from himself alone and not from the consent of the church" (*ex sese, non ex consensu ecclesiae*).[26] Within a pyramidal framework this seems to turn the pope into an absolute despot and reduce the bishops to mere deputies. No Catholic theologian went quite that far, but many did think that the need for councils was eliminated because it was now clear that the pope could do by himself the very things for which councils were formerly convoked.[27]

However, now that the essential structure of the church is declared to be collegial, not monarchical, these extreme, absolutistic affirmations of papal authority must be modified. To put it over-simply, they now can be understood as referring not to powers which the pope should normally exercise but to powers which he may assume in an emergency. I am using an analogy from the political realm, but it does have some applicability. Under unusual circumstances such as war, the President of the United States acquires many dictatorial powers, but because the fundamental constitution of the country is democratic, these are relinquished in normal times. It is in some such way that the papal supremacy of the First Vatican Council is reconcilable with the collegiality affirmed by the Second.

In the light of this principle of collegiality, the papalism and the Roman centralism which have developed over many centuries constitute abnormal ways of governing the church. Now that greater theological insight and changing historical circumstances have made this apparent, many Roman Catholics think it is time to return to organizational structures which are more appropriate to the fundamentally collegial character of the church and better adapted to modern times. If the vision of the church as the col-

[26] DS No. 3074.
[27] E.g., the canonist P. Hinschius, claimed in 1883 that "the general council has become unnecessary and superfluous for the Catholic Church. Since the Vaticanum it no longer has any independent legal significance alongside the papacy." Quoted by K. E. Skydsgaard, "The Coming Council, Its Purpose and Problems," in *The Papal Council and the Gospel, op. cit.*, p. 95.

legially structured people of God is actualized, it will mean that the role of the pope will become rather like that of the United States Supreme Court. He will act chiefly when disputes are referred to him which have proved impossible to settle in other ways. Even an Italian cardinal such as Lercaro, one of the four moderators of the Council, has proposed that the parts of the church would become "autocephalous"[28] and that the task of the pope would be not so much to rule as to act as a guardian of unity by serving as a final court of appeal.

This does not contradict Vatican I because the judgments of the pope would be final and therefore, from the juridical point of view, effective "of themselves and not because of the consent of others."[29] Yet, as in the case of any final court of appeal such as the Supreme Court, this would not make the pope anything remotely resembling an absolute monarch because the circumstances under which he would exercise this ultimate authority would be severely limited.

One objection which might loom large from our present perspective would not, I suspect, be very important in the long run. The pope, in the light of the decrees of Vatican I, would remain the sole judge of when to assume emergency powers and when to relinquish them.[30] Anyone, however, who knows the enormous pressure which precedent, custom, and established tradition exert in a large community such as the Roman Catholic Church will be inclined to agree that any arbitrary assumption of emergency powers without the *de facto,* even if not formal, consent of the

28 In a speech at the Greek College in Rome during the third session of the Council. Cf. also n. 10, p. 82 above.

29 This formula is widely described as misleading by contemporary Roman Catholic writers. It was directed against the Gallican thesis that papal definitions required the formally expressed consent of the bishops in order to be binding. What Vatican I declares, therefore, is that the pope can act independently of such formal consent, but not that he can act independently of the *sensus ecclesiae* or *contra consensum ecclesiae.* Cf. R. Aubert, "L'ecclesiologie au concile du Vatican," in *Le concile et les conciles,* ed. O. Rousseau (Chevetogne: Éditions de Chevetogne, 1960), p. 281; and Küng, *Structures of the Church, op. cit.,* p. 375.

30 It should be noted that what we are calling "emergency" powers may at the same time be "ordinary" in the technical language employed by Vatican I. "Ordinary" powers are those which inhere in an office and are exercised at the discretion of the officeholder, even if he in fact rarely or never employs them. G. Thils, *Primauté pontificale et prérogatives épiscopales* (Louvain, 1961), pp. 98–99.

church is most unlikely once collegial procedures are well established. Recent popes have had the utmost difficulty in breaking out of the limits set by curial traditions. Pope John is reported to have said "I am in a bag here."[31] He had to convoke a council to help him escape.

In addition to the weight of an established collegial order, there might even be recognized doctrinal and canonical provisions in the church of the future against arbitrary papal action. Any pope who needlessly and destructively overturned the collegial structures would, presumably, be either mentally deranged or else unbalanced in morals or in faith in such a way as to be schismatic or heretical.[32] Such a pope, according to the canonical provisions which were accepted in the Middle Ages and according to the decree *Haec sancta* of the Council of Constance (which an increasing number of Roman Catholic scholars insist remains juridically binding), can be deposed. It is no secret that as a matter of fact there were a number of papal depositions during those troubled centuries which are still recognized as legitimate by the Roman Church. They were carried out, in some cases at least, by men who had views of the authority of the Petrine office basically identical with those of Vatican I, and who were in no sense acting against the office but against the persons of men unworthy to hold that office.[33]

But even if the papal system were protected against abuses as completely as is possible by human ecclesiastical provisions, and even if the Roman Catholic Church were governed with as much or more effective democracy than most Protestant denominations, the sons of the Reformation would still not be satisfied. They would object, as we have already mentioned, that there are no adequate grounds, no scriptural grounds, for supposing that the Petrine office is the God-willed center of catholic unity and that all churches which are not in communion with it are institutionally defective.

---

[31] Kaiser, *Pope, Council and World, op. cit.*, p. 10.
[32] For a discussion of these and other possible ways in which a pope can cease to be pope, and the need for a council to confirm this cessation, see Küng, *Structures of the Church, op. cit.*, pp. 257–68.
[33] A. Franzen, "The Council of Constance: Present State of the Problem," in *Historical Problems of Church Renewal*, Vol. VII of *Concilium, op. cit.* (1965), pp. 29–68.

In moments of speculative fancy I can imagine modifications of the Roman Catholic understanding of what is meant by "divine institution" which would overcome this objection. Such changes have already occurred, for example, in reference to the dogma of the dominical institution of the seven sacraments. Some writers have suggested that dominical institution, at least in the case of some of the sacraments, simply means that they developed historically in post-biblical times under God's providential guidance as an explication and articulation of the proto-sacrament, which is the church.[34] If the papacy were divinely instituted in an analogous way, then one could say, so to speak, that it is a matter both of divine and human law. This would make it similar to the Israelite monarchy which, according to I Samuel 8, was the result both of historical circumstances which prompted the demands of the people, and of God's appointment. He reluctantly approved an historical development resulting in part from the people's unfaithfulness. Perhaps in a similar way the successors of the apostle Peter, like the successors of King David in the days of old, have a place in the church by what might be called divine as well as human institution.

However, there would still be disagreement on what that place is. The sons of the Reformation would continue to insist on the right and obligation to a kind of prophetic resistance to tyranny which the kings of Israel were reluctant to acknowledge and which there is no indication that the Church of Rome would ever be able to allow. That church seems permanently committed to a principle of dogmatic infallibility which excludes the possibility of admitting that popes and councils have ever erred in such a way as to justify a protest like the Protestant one. Indeed, the very self-identity of Rome seems to depend on its maintaining this conviction. And, conversely, the self-identity of Protestantism depends on its insistence that the Reformation break in the unity of the church, despite its tragedy, was legitimate and necessary in faithfulness to the gospel. Reunion seems excluded, and only surrender by one side or another appears to be a possible way to unity. In short, the rock on which the confessions seem perma-

[34] Rahner, *The Church and the Sacraments, op. cit.,* pp. 41–74.

ECUMENISM AND STRUCTURES

nently split is not so much papacy as infallibility and, even more precisely, who was right and who was wrong in the sixteenth century.

Yet, despite the absence of any glimmer of insight in the documents of Vatican II on how to solve this ultimate issue, it would be foolish of Protestants to underestimate what Roman Catholics are now attempting. For the first time since the early centuries of the church, we see the beginnings of an effort to combine genuine ecclesiastical authority in a communion of vast size and diversity with ordered freedom and extensive lay participation. Our Protestant failures to reconcile liberty and authority naturally make us skeptical of this experiment, but it would be folly to deny that it may succeed. In the realm of secular politics, most of us are convinced that it is a serious error to think that strong government is necessarily tyrannical, necessarily undemocratic. We think that there is a vast difference between Washington and Moscow even though both are centers of immense power. We are opposed to "states'-righters." We point out that extensive and powerful governmental action is often necessary in order to supply those needs for justice, material goods, and peace which are prerequisites for freedom. We acknowledge that modern communications, together with the development of organizational devices such as representative government and the division and balancing of legislative, executive, and judicial powers, make it possible to operate democracies of vastly greater size and stability than was possible for the ancient Greeks for whom the only choice was between small free cities and gigantic Oriental despotisms. It is, therefore, strange that we should dogmatically deny that something analogous is possible in the ecclesiastical domain. Of course we do not know whether the Roman Church will succeed in substantially "democratizing" its structures, but we must at least reckon with the possibility. It is conceivable that we shall in the future be confronted by a Roman Catholicism which allows for Protestant liberty but does not have Protestant divisiveness and institutional weakness and inertia.

If this were to happen, Rome would be leading the way in showing how the church should be organized in order effectively

95

to foster *koinonia* and carry out its mission. This gives special urgency to the question of whether union without surrender of self-identity on either side is perhaps possible after all; and it is for this reason that we turn in the next chapter to a consideration of the greatest obstacle to unity: the conflict between Roman claims to infallibility for its dogmatic traditions and the Reformation's insistence on the *sola scriptura*.

5

CATHOLIC DOGMA
AND THE WORD OF GOD

We suggested in the last chapter that, within the new perspectives emerging at Vatican II, the ultimate theological obstacle to the unity and *koinonia* of the church is not the problem of ecclesiastical structures, not even the problem of the papacy, but the debate over the infallibility of the church's dogmas versus the *sola scriptura*. What is the final norm of the church's life and mission? Both sides agree that it is that revelation of God which culminates in Jesus Christ, but they differ on how the ultimately authoritative public knowledge of that revelation is transmitted to us. Roman Catholics maintain that it comes not solely through Scripture but also through traditions and dogmas which the church is competent to define as infallible, while Protestants insist on Scripture alone.

From this it appears that our consideration of the theology of the Council here reaches its climax. The question of Christian unity is at stake, not merely in reference to some hypothetical and as yet invisible goal of final unification, but in the sense of increasing cooperation in concrete ways in the present and immediate future. To the extent that Catholics and Protestants are able to recognize each other as genuinely striving to be faithful to the same Lord, to the Christ testified to in the Bible, they will find it possible to join forces as signs and agents of reconciliation in the world.

In this chapter, therefore, we shall successively consider both the progress and the limits of the current movement in Catholicism away from dependence on magisterial infallibility towards greater reliance on Scripture. Finally, we shall examine the implications of this for the churches of the Reformation.

I

The role of dogmatic infallibility is transformed, even though not denied, when it is interpreted within the framework of the new understanding of the world and the church. Its function seems to become that of safeguarding the unity of the church rather than of supplying information or guidance for the theological understanding of revelation.[1]

This change becomes intelligible when one considers the close connection between traditional conceptions of dogma and the static, two-story, classical universe. In the older perspective, revelation was thought of chiefly as the communication of propositions or of eternal truths in the form of statements to the human mind. The propositional truths contained in the Bible or, in some cases, in the oral tradition were identical with revelation. This made it possible to conceive of doctrinal formulations as directly continuous with revelation, as summaries of or compelling deductions from revealed truths.[2]

Further, these formulations were supposed to be permanently valid, intelligible, and relevant. Once a doctrine was properly stated and explained, there was no need ever to change the mode of expression. Human nature and human intelligence were thought to be sufficiently unchanging so that it was possible to discover an enduringly adequate way of thinking, that of the perennial philosophy, especially as expounded by St. Thomas Aquinas. If

---

[1] This is the argument of my article, "Reform and Infallibility," *Cross Currents*, XI (1961), 345–56.

[2] Not only Roman Catholics but also scholastic Protestants of the seventeenth century and later thought in these terms. The two groups disagreed mainly over the question of whether knowledge of revelation came only from Scripture or was supplemented, as the Catholics held, by information transmitted through the oral tradition. For a good summary of the Protestant position, see W. Pannenberg, "Was ist eine dogmatische Aussage?" *Pro Veritate*, ed. E. Schlink and H. Wolf (Münster: Aschendorff'sche Verlagsbuchhandlung, 1963), pp. 339–61, esp. pp. 343–46.

one used its categories, doctrinal formulations could be made exempt from the ravages of time.[3]

Such convictions become untenable once creation is viewed as in process and human nature is conceived of as an essentially historical reality in which unpredictably surprising potentialities are constantly being actualized. Dogmas can no longer be thought of as changelessly adequate embodiments of revealed eternal truths, for such embodiments do not exist. Historical studies have made Catholics as well as non-Catholics intensely aware of the time-conditioned and culture-conditioned character of all human language, even when it is used by the church. Meaning depends on the situation, and to repeat abiding truths in the same old ways in radically new circumstances is not to preserve, but to betray them. The only way to say the same thing in a new context is to say it differently.[4]

This change of outlook was expressly recognized and approved by the Council. Indeed, it already received official endorsement in what was rightly noted as perhaps the most important passage in Pope John's opening speech when he said that the unchanging substance of the deposit of faith needs to be formulated in new ways.[5]

The very notion of revelation is altered in the new outlook. According to the conciliar Constitution on Divine Revelation, revelation is not propositional, but consists of "deeds," of God's acts in history (art. 2), especially as these are "perfected" in Jesus' death and resurrection (art. 4). It is true, the document adds, that the words which provide an explanation of the significance of these mighty deeds also play a constitutive part in revelation, but they do this in "inner unity" with the events. Thus the Council has in effect adopted that view of the nature of revelation which has been developed and popularized in recent times by what is often called "neo-orthodoxy," but which in this

---

[3] An influential example of this position is provided by R. Garrigou-Lagrange, *De Revelatione* (Rome: Ferrari, 1929).

[4] "Heresy is possible . . . not merely through the denial of already fixed formulae of faith, but also through the rigid clinging to these formulae in a new confessional situation. . . ." W. Kasper, "The Relationship Between Gospel and Dogma," in *Man as Man and Believer, op. cit.,* p. 157.

[5] *The Documents of Vatican II, op. cit.,* p. 715.

respect can lay claim to being a revival of the oldest orthodoxy, that of the Bible itself.[6]

The implications of this are immense, opening up the possibility of what can without exaggeration be called the "reform," though not the "abrogation" or "replacement," of dogmas. Because revelation centers in events, not propositions, doctrinal formulations can no longer be thought of as deductions from or summaries of its contents. Rather, they must be understood as necessarily inadequate and partial efforts to understand and interpret the mysteries of faith. Even an infallible dogma can be poorly balanced or incomplete in its statement. Consequently it might actually be misleading, particularly if simply repeated in new contexts without explanatory additions. Some influential Roman Catholic theologians have suggested that this is true even of the Trinitarian and Christological formulations of the early church.[7] The Council cites no examples, but it does encourage such reflections by speaking in one memorable phrase in the Decree on Ecumenism of "deficiencies . . . even in the formulation of doctrine" which need to be "rectified" (art. 6).

This may seem like an abandonment of the "infallibility" and, more especially, the "irreformability" of dogma, but actually these terms retain a definite, though altered, meaning in the new theological outlook. It is not so much that the formulation itself is irreformable as that the dogmatic decision of which it is the expression is irreversible. When the church decides a theological question, it chooses rightly among the various practically possible alternatives available at the time. It may appear from a later perspective that none of these alternatives was particularly fortunate and that even the one chosen needs badly to be supplemented by further decisions rectifying abuses and misunderstandings. Nevertheless, the original choice still stands as, at the very least,

---

[6] In his commentary, J. Ratzinger says that this basic concept of revelation in the Constitution on Revelation incorporates the stimuli coming from the theological developments between the First and Second World Wars, but "leaves out of consideration the recent controversy between a theology of Heilsgeschichte (Cullmann) and a Worttheologie (Bultmann, Ebeling)." *Lexikon für Theologie und Kirche. Das Zweite Vatikanische Konzil, op. cit.,* II, 507–8.

[7] E.g., K. Rahner, "Current Problems in Christology," *Theological Investigations, op. cit.,* I, 149–200.

capable of being given an interpretation which is without actual error or which is reconcilable with the truth.[8] It is in some such fashion as this, so the outside observer is inclined to think, that some Roman Catholic theologians now regard the sixteenth-century decision about justification, for example. This was correct, they seem to argue, not because the Tridentine doctrine of justification is better than that of the Reformers—on the contrary, the Reformers were in some respects closer to the truth—but because, in the concrete situation of that day, acceptance of the Reformation position would have necessarily involved embracing irretrievably serious errors on other matters such as the church.[9]

This might be called the "decision theory" of doctrinal development. It is obviously quite different, not only from the classical deductive theories, but also from the cumulative, organic growth theories which derive from Cardinal Newman. Contrary to these, it denies that the church's understanding of the faith grows continuously and progressively through the addition of new dogmas, and rather affirms that it needs to be constantly reformulated and corrected in the light of changing circumstances and renewed attention to the sources of the faith.

This does not mean that there are no advances of any sort in the understanding of the faith. It means rather that whatever development there is must be understood not as analogous to a process of cumulative growth or unfolding in which later phases are germinally present and naturally surpass the earlier, but rather as similar to the much weaker type of "progress" in comprehension which comes from viewing the same object from different perspectives as one moves away, around, or towards it.[10]

It is difficult to avoid the conclusion that views such as this

8 "Many dogmas after their proclamation often go through a complicated and frequently astonishing process of interpretation before their real meaning becomes clear." Kasper, *op. cit.*, p. 160.

9 This is what seems to be implied, though not explicitly stated, by H. Küng, *Justification: The Doctrine of Karl Barth and a Catholic Reflection* (New York: Thomas Nelson & Sons, 1964). His views have received wide acceptance among Catholics.

10 For a fuller development of the contrast between these two views of the development of doctrine, see G. Lindbeck, "Doctrinal Development and Contemporary Protestant Theology," in *Man as Man and Believer*, *op. cit.*, pp. 133–49.

will become standard in the future.[11] A decision theory of doctrinal development is not only demanded by the pervasive awareness of the historically conditioned character of knowledge and speech, but also supported by the realistically eschatological conviction that God wills the vast transmutations which humanity experiences in the course of time. The church must always be open to God's future. Who knows what indescribable insights may open up in the next few thousand years, if mankind endures that long? It may be that all our most treasured theological formulas, both Catholic and Protestant, will be replaced, even if not denied, by other ways of describing that incomprehensible mystery of God's love in Jesus Christ from which and to which we move.[12]

However, it should not be supposed that this attitude towards doctrinal development is explicitly developed in the Council documents. The strength of the traditional mentality was still too strong. Actually the language which is most often used, especially in an extended passage in the Constitution on Divine Revelation (art. 8), is that of a Newmanian cumulative, organic growth theory which is appropriate not for a pilgrim-people ecclesiology but for a body-of-Christ, continuation-of-the-incarnation view of the church.[13]

Nevertheless, the actions of the Council point in the direction of what we are calling the decision theory. Even Paul VI, in his first speech to the Council after he became pope, suggested that collegiality is a corrective of the "fear wrongly deduced" from the papal dogmas of Vatican I.[14] A more trenchant example is the Declaration on Religious Freedom which reversed a tradition of magisterial teaching so massive that many Roman Catholic theologians, as well as bishops in council, argued that the church could

[11] See, for example, G. Baum, "Doctrinal Renewal," *Journal of Ecumenical Studies*, II (1965), 365–81, esp. 375–78.

[12] The eschatological emphasis on the incomplete, provisional, future-directed character of all doctrinal formulations is particularly strong in what are perhaps the two best recent Catholic discussions of the nature of dogma: W. Kasper, *Dogma unter dem Wort Gottes* (Mainz: Matthias-Grünewald Verlag, 1965); and K. Rahner and K. Lehmann, "Kerygma und Dogma," *Mysterium Salutis* (Einsiedeln: Benziger Verlag, 1965), I, 622–703.

[13] The most incisive and balanced Protestant critique of the Constitution on Revelation is that of K. E. Skydsgaard, "Scripture and Tradition," in *Challenge and Response, op. cit.*, pp. 25–28.

[14] X. Rynne, *The Second Session* (New York: Farrar & Straus, 1964), p. 349.

not reverse itself on this point.[15] The Constitution on the Liturgy provides several examples of the profound modification and correction, even if not formal contradiction or repeal, of conciliar decisions made in the past.[16] Birth control, despite its recent reaffirmation by Paul VI in *Humanae vita,* may still eventually provide another illustration of a change in a position which, although never formally defined, had the practical force of dogma in recent times.[17] Perhaps the clearest illustration of all is the virtual reversal on the possibility of salvation outside the church.[18]

It is clear that these changes in the official teaching of the church are drastically altering the traditional Roman Catholic view of magisterial authority.[19] The magisterium can no longer be thought of, as it so often was in the context of a pyramidal, institution-of-salvation ecclesiology, as having special access to divine truth. It is dependent on the same sources of knowledge as are theologians and laymen. The special assistance promised to the magisterium when it is exercising its official teaching function sometimes seems to amount to no more than the guarantee that it will not fall into irremediable error. Even relatively conservative Catholics have to admit that this kind of preventive action was all the Spirit was able to manage in the darker periods of the Middle Ages or at the time of the Reformation. In view of this more sober estimate of the doctrinal competence of the church's leadership, there is greater emphasis on theological di-

---

15 A good example of this kind of argument is provided by the Council speech of Cardinal de Arriba y Castro, archbishop of Tarragona, on Sept. 15, 1965, reprinted in *Die Autorität der Freiheit, op. cit.,* III, 195–97. The counterargument, emphasizing the development of doctrine, was presented to the Council most fully by Bishop De Smedt of Bruges in his "relatio" during the second session; reprinted in *Council Speeches of Vatican II, op. cit.,* esp. pp. 246–53.

16 For example, in its encouragement of the use of the vernacular, of Communion in two kinds, and of communal (e.g., concelebrated) masses.

17 G. Baum, "Is the Church's Position on Birth Control Infallible?" *The Ecumenist,* IV (1964), 83–85. The basic argument of conservatives as expressed in the report by the papal commission on this subject is that the church has expressed itself too clearly and authoritatively to be able to change in the way the progressives advocate. For the text, see *National Catholic Reporter,* April 19, 1967, pp. 9–11.

18 Compare, e.g., the teaching of the Council of Florence, DS No. 1351, with that of Vatican II as expressed in C 15 and 16, CMW 22, and E and NCR *passim.*

19 E.g., G. Baum, "The Magisterium in a Changing Church," in *Man as Man and Believer, op. cit.,* pp. 67–83.

versity and freedom in the church and on the roles of laymen[20] as well as theologians in the interpretation of the deposit of faith. Once again, however, the Council does not explicitly emphasize this point. Indeed, in one place in the Constitution on Revelation it seems to say the opposite. "The task of authentically interpreting the word of God," it says, "has been entrusted exclusively to the living teaching office of the Church" (art. 10). To be sure, this "exclusively" needs to be understood in the light of a later passage from the same document where it is explained that although "interpreting Scripture is subject finally to the judgment of the Church," preparatory studies are still necessary so that this "judgment of the Church may mature" (art. 12). At this point as at many others, however, the actual practice of the Council was more eloquent than its words. One of the Protestant observers officially delegated to the Council commented privately that the bishops did not seem to be at all sure even of their collective infallibility and that this helps account for the enthusiasm with which they followed John XXIII's proposal to keep this a pastoral council which formulated no new dogmas.

Yet it would be a mistake to suppose, as some Protestants as well as Catholics are eager to do, that this development threatens to eviscerate infallibility and make it an empty and hypocritical shibboleth. Within the context of a decision theory of doctrinal development, infallibility acquires, as already suggested, the decisively important function of safeguarding the unity of the church.[21] We have seen that in the new historical framework of thought dogmas can be inopportune, unbalanced, and dangerously misunderstood, perhaps even by those involved in their promulgation, yet it is still firmly insisted that the Holy Spirit sees to it that they are not irretrievably erroneous. The errors they clearly and specifically exclude are in fact errors, and their positive affirmations are capable of being given an interpretation in conformity to revealed truth even though, as a matter of fact, such a correct interpretation may not yet have been properly formulated. Consequently, the faithful Catholic does not leave the

[20] Das Dynamische in der Kirche (Freiburg: Herder & Co., 1958), p. 39.
[21] For this paragraph, see the article cited in n. 1, p. 98 above.

Roman Church or shatter its unity even when he is not at all
sure of the sense in which a given dogma is true and even when
he is vigorously opposed to the way in which it is interpreted
by theologians and the ordinary magisterium. He believes that
some acceptable interpretation can be found and that God has
not allowed the church to proclaim a flatly erroneous dogma. It
is because of such considerations that Hans Küng can write:

Perhaps the day will come when it will be fully recognized that although the term "infallibility" does indeed express the binding force
of the formulations of faith, it does not indicate their fragmentary
character. With this in mind perhaps a concept will then be found
which, better than the term "infallibility," will present in an encom-
passing and balanced manner the strict binding force of decrees and at
the same time their profoundly incomplete character.[22]

In short, the church must be able to make binding decisions on
questions which threaten its unity, and these decisions are never
so inadequate that they must be rejected, but they are in no
sense sacrosanct supplements to revealed truth and are subject
to constant review, supplementation, and interpretation.

Such an interpretation of infallibility would come close to—
although it would not be identical with—what the Eastern Orthodox and perhaps some Protestants think is implied by the indefectibility of the church. This point is suggested by certain formulations of Karl Rahner. The offices of the church, he says, do not
have the "same quality of eschatological indefectibility" as does
the church as a whole.[23] The leaders and teachers of the church
can fail, they can even act against the church in some sense, but
never in such a way as to destroy the indefectibility of the church
itself. That is, "the offices of the church cannot be used as weap-
ons against God in the most real and essential sense," for it is
not possible that the church should ever forfeit its truth and its
love by acts of the offices instituted by Christ.[24] The view of the
Eastern Orthodox would appear to be similar, except that they

[22] *Journal of Ecumenical Studies,* I (1964), 111.
[23] "Kirche und Parusie Christi," *Schriften zur Theologie, op. cit.,* VI, 360.
[24] "Kirche und Parusie Christi," *op. cit.,* p. 362. When stated precisely,
magisterial infallibility simply excludes the possibility "that the supreme teaching and pastoral office of the church would ever make use in respect to the
whole church of its highest teaching and pastoral power by which it ultimately

would add two crucial qualifications. First, it is the universal church, not simply the Roman portion, which is guaranteed against accepting doctrine which vitally threatens Christian truth. Second, to the Eastern Orthodox the sign of doctrinal infallibility, of the lack of fundamental error, is not only that a decision has been promulgated by the juridically competent authorities, but also that it has been received by the church as a whole.[25]

The gap between the two positions is still considerable, but there is one further consideration which makes it at least theologically conceivable that Roman Catholics and Orthodox might some day reach agreement without either side capitulating to the other. The Decree on Ecumenism says: "When comparing doctrines," Roman Catholic theologians "should remember that in Catholic teaching there exists an order or 'hierarchy' of truths, since they vary in their relationship to the foundation of the Christian faith" (art. 11). The drafters of this document, in explaining the reasons for this recommendation, state:

It seems to be of the greatest importance for the ecumenical dialogue that both the truths in which Christians agree and those in which they differ should be weighed rather than counted. Although all revealed truths are undoubtedly to be held by divine faith, their importance and "weight" differ according to their connection with the history of salvation and the mystery of Christ.[26]

obligates and binds all, in such a way as to contradict the truth and the saving will of Christ so that the reception and following of such an act would set the whole church in its entirety in unequivocal contradiction to Christ, that is, in an error so absolute as to be a 'no' to his truth or a 'no' to his reconciling and saving love." *Ibid.*

Even from the point of view of staunch Protestants, it is not at all clear that the Roman magisterium has ever committed an error of this kind. The Marian and papal dogmas are capable of being interpreted, as current efforts show, in such a way that it would be difficult indeed to prove that they are "unequivocally" opposed to Christ's truth and love in the sense indicated by the above quotation. Given so limited a definition of infallibility and the vast possibilities of reinterpretation and correction of earlier dogmas which it implies, the Protestant can no longer argue that any of the Roman dogmas are in fact in error in the drastically strong sense which Rahner proposes. The Protestant's objection is reduced to the single point that there is no divine guarantee against the possibility of the church's teaching office falling into such an error sometime. This, to be sure, is a crucial disagreement.

[25] The Orthodox are not unanimous on this point. Y. Congar gives numerous references to those holding a stronger view of conciliar infallibility in *Le concile et les conciles, op. cit.,* p. 288, n. 2.

[26] Cited in *Lexikon für Theologie und Kirche. Das Zweite Vatikanische Konzil, op. cit.,* II, 89, n. 48.

This immediately raises the question of whether the Roman Catholic Church might conceivably at some future time rate the papal and Marian dogmas which are peculiar to it so low in the hierarchy of truths, so remote from the central Christological dogmas, that it would ask other churches simply not to deny them or to accept them as legitimate optional theological opinions rather than as dogmas which must be affirmed.[27] Is it possible that this might someday be considered a sufficient doctrinal consensus for the re-establishment of full ecclesiastical communion? The Roman Catholics would in addition doubtless insist on arrangements for governing and preserving the unity of the church which would include the "practical" primacy of the Petrine See at least in the sense of a final court of appeal as described in the last chapter. But it is at least an open question whether they are dogmatically committed to insisting that the non-Latin churches of the East accept this primacy as part of revealed truth, as *de iure divino,* in the sense implied by Vatican I.

These are not altogether fantastic speculations. A partial precedent has already been supplied by the Council of Florence (1438–39) which agreed to a union between East and West without demanding that the Greeks insert the *filioque* in the Creed.[28] In view of the intensity and character of the new Roman Catholic ecumenism, it seems quite possible that these questions will soon

[27] One of the members of the Vatican's Secretariat for the Promotion of Christian Unity has spelled out the "hierarchy of truths" in this way: "Grace has more importance than sin, sanctifying grace more than actual grace, the Holy Spirit more than Our Lady, the resurrection of Christ more than his childhood, the mystical aspect of the Church more than its juridical, the Church's liturgy more than private devotions, baptism more than penance, the Eucharist more than the anointing of sick." T. Stransky, "The Separated Churches and Ecclesial Communities," in *Vatican II on Ecumenism,* ed. M. Adams (Dublin, 1967), p. 55.

[28] J. Gill, *The Council of Florence* (Cambridge: Cambridge University Press, 1959). It can be argued that the parallel is not exact, for both parties at Florence affirmed that it was one and the same belief which was expressed by the creed, despite the difference in formulation. W. Kasper, however, claims that the difference was irreducible because of the radical diversity in the Eastern and Western thought forms (*Stimmen der Zeit,* CLXXIX [1967], 401–16). If this is true, then the Florentine solution was identical to the one here proposed in which divided churches acknowledge each other's peculiar beliefs as admissible theological positions, but not as binding dogmas. In practice, this acknowledgment would presumably have to come from the non-Catholics, because it is the Roman Church which has dogmas additional to

be publicly discussed, as they already are privately. And if this happens the churches of the Reformation will have to take some stand in reference to them. This could be a grave embarrassment, for while most Protestants would be averse to these terms of union, they are not historically committed to rejecting them. It could be argued that the Appendix to the Smalcald articles, for example, lays down conditions for reunion whose fundamental intention is similar to what Roman Catholics may soon begin discussing. This is the reason we have raised this seemingly far-fetched issue of whether even the barrier of infallible dogmas might be surmountable in the new theological context.

II

The churches of the Reformation, however, are concerned not primarily with polemicizing against infallibility but with affirming the *sola scriptura*. It is quite possible, as various kinds of sectarians and theological liberals have done, to reject dogmatic and magisterial authority without thereby becoming more biblical. Roman Catholics, like all of us, are tempted to substitute for the shackles of traditionalism not obedience to the revelatory word but subservience to the idols of modernity, relevance, and pragmatic success.

It is true that in the aftermath of the Council vast numbers of Catholics are yielding to these temptations. This is scarcely a criticism of Vatican II, however, as Protestants in particular should be quick to recognize in view of the sectarianism and divisiveness which was occasioned, even if not caused, by the Reformation. Our concern, however, is not with the popular ferment, important though that is for the church, but with the theological developments reflected in the conciliar documents.

It is no exaggeration to say that these developments have been in the direction of the *sola scriptura*. Indeed, the words themselves

those accepted by the Orthodox and retained by the Reformers. Cf. Avery Dulles, "Dogma as an Ecumenical Problem," *Theological Studies*, XXIX (1968), 403–4.

have become a slogan in some contemporary Roman Catholic circles.[29] The phrase *"in ora ecclesiae"* is added, but this supplement, if understood in a certain way, is one which Protestants can accept. The so-called "right to private interpretation" has no place in the central Reformation tradition. Scripture should always be read and interpreted in the community of believers. Karl Barth has correctly pointed out that the man who does not pay serious attention to the exegesis of fellow Christians—including that of other epochs and other communions—is in effect refusing full submission to the authority of Scripture and to the Holy Spirit who is its interpreter.

This does not mean that Roman Catholics and Protestants understand the *sola scriptura* in identical ways, but rather that it is becoming increasingly difficult to find neat formulas with which to mark the difference. First of all, "Scripture alone" versus "Scripture and tradition" is no longer adequate. Most Roman Catholics now writing on the subject[30] maintain what is called the "material sufficiency" of Scripture. Tradition, they say, is not a second, supplementary source of information about revelation, but rather hermeneutical, the medium in and through which the truths witnessed to by the Bible are transmitted and interpreted. In this sense of *paradosis,* of handing on, tradition is the lifestream of the church, and the formula by which the Council of Trent "receives and honors" Scripture and tradition "with an equal affection of piety and reverence" (DS No. 1501) becomes unobjectionable. This theory of "one source" of the knowledge of revelation is similar in its broad outlines to the view of Scripture and tradition which has become current in many Protestant circles in recent decades.

Contemporary Roman Catholics are affirming not only the mate-

[29] The fullest and best Protestant treatment of recent Roman Catholic considerations of the authority of Scripture is G. C. Berkouwer, *The Second Vatican Council and the New Catholicism* (Grand Rapids, Mich.: Eerdmans, 1965), pp. 89–145, 163–77.

[30] E.g., J. R. Geiselmann, *The Meaning of Tradition* (New York: Herder & Herder, 1966); K. Rahner and J. Ratzinger, *Revelation and Tradition* (Herder & Herder, 1966); G. Tavard, *Holy Writ or Holy Church* (London: Burns & Oates, 1959).

rial sufficiency of the Bible but also its normativeness. Yves Congar, whom Pope Paul has described as his favorite among living theologians, sounds thoroughly Protestant when he writes that "Scripture is absolutely sovereign," with the implication that it is the norm for tradition and not the other way around.[31] Rahner does not hesitate to appropriate what Protestants have thought of as the strongest possible expression of the authority of the Bible: it is the *"norma normans, non normata* of both dogmatic and non-dogmatic statements of faith."[32]

Protestants are puzzled by such affirmations because they seem irreconcilable with magisterial infallibility. Even when magisterial infallibility is qualified in the ways sketched in the previous section, it leaves the Roman Catholic willing to acquiesce to dogmas which have no explicit foundation in the Bible, which cannot be plausibly represented as interpretive traditions. The Catholic response that these dogmas are implicitly present in Scripture does not satisfy the Protestant critic, because even when he is willing to admit that certain doctrines which he accepts, such as the Trinitarian one, are only implicitly in the Bible, he argues that they represent the only conceivable answer harmonizable with the biblical witness to certain questions which have been posed in the course of time. For example, when the church was forced to choose between the Arian contention that the Son is merely a creature and the Nicean affirmation that he is *homoousion*, consubstantial, with the Father, it could only answer *homoousion* if it was to be faithful to the scriptural witness that it is God himself who is our Redeemer. This kind of direct biblical foundation is absent in the case of the peculiarly Roman dogmas. They cannot be plausibly represented as the *only* answers consistent with the Bible to the questions to which they were addressed.[33] More than that, in the words of Oscar Cullmann, commenting on the Council's statement on Mary, "if the bodily Assumption of Mary

[31] *La Tradition et les traditions* (Paris: Cerf, 1963), II, 177.

[32] "What Is a Dogmatic Statement?" *Theological Investigations, op. cit.,* V, 64. "Exegesis and Dogmatic Theology," *ibid.,* pp. 67–93, is also relevant.

[33] For the argument of this paragraph, see my article cited in n. 10, p. 101 above.

really is implicitly in the Bible, then I really don't know what is *not* implicitly in the Bible."[34]

Even though this Roman Catholic form of the *norma normans, non normata* does not satisfy the Protestant, we must recognize that it makes a profound difference to the work of the theologians who accept it. It means, so at least the outside observer finds himself inclined to say, that the traditional procedure of interpreting the Bible in the light of dogma is reversed; instead, dogma is interpreted in terms of Scripture. It is not assumed that dogma is clear and Scripture obscure; rather the relation is often the opposite, and the way to find the true meaning for today of the dogmas which are incomprehensible or distorted is to interpret them within a framework of understanding derived from Scripture and validated by Scripture. We have already seen numerous examples of this: for example, the argument that the papal office must be understood within the context of the biblical vision of the messianic pilgrim people rather than of a unilaterally monarchical institution of salvation. The Marian dogmas could also be cited as an illustration, for these are sometimes given an interpretation so evangelical (in the Reformation sense of the word) that it is conceivable that the Reformers themselves would have admitted them as possible pious opinions, though not as dogmas.[35] Thus, for an influential and growing group of Catholic theologians the Bible is not at all the mere collection of proof texts which the scholastic tradition so often made it; it is rather the independently normative source and guide to the understanding of all that pertains to revelation, including the church's doctrinal decisions.

As we have seen time and again in our discussion, the conciliar documents reflect only the first stages of this movement of thought. The passages in the Constitution on Divine Revelation (arts. 7–10) which deal with the nature and relation of Scripture and tradition, for example, are a masterpiece of ambiguity. They say everything and nothing. They were quite deliberately framed, as the publicly known history of the Council makes clear, in order

---

[34] "The Bible in the Council," in *Dialogue on the Way, op. cit.,* p. 134.
[35] E.g., by Rahner, *Theological Investigations, op. cit.,* I, 201–27.

to avoid making any decisions between the traditional two-source theory of revelation and the newer one-source theory which affirms the material sufficiency of Scripture.[36] However, this in fact gives a great impetus to the one-source view because, to a far greater degree than ever before, the magisterium has used formulations which are congenial to that view. Reviving an old theme, it says that biblical study is the "soul of sacred theology" (art. 24) and "like the Christian religion itself, all the preaching of the Church must be nourished and ruled by sacred Scripture" (art. 21). Further, the Bible should be the primary source for all religious instruction, and should constantly be studied by everyone, including the laity (arts. 22, 25).

It is safe to predict that the present trend towards increasing reliance on the Bible will continue in Roman Catholic theology. This is true in part simply because nothing else is feasible within the new historical framework of understanding. Because revelation is primarily a matter of events, knowledge of it is transmitted chiefly through the scriptural stories of God's saving acts and promises and the biblical images by which they are explained. Formal abstract theological and doctrinal propositions simply cannot be considered, as once they were in a classically intellectualist outlook, as capable of containing revealed truth. Now they become nothing more than secondary and changeable protective devices and commentaries.

Further, the historical mode of scriptural study and exegesis which is appropriate to this new outlook has been firmly approved by the Council. To be sure, the Constitution on Divine Revelation asserts the inerrancy of the Bible in reference to those truths which are "for the sake of our salvation" (art. 11), but it does this in such a way as to allow virtually unlimited freedom to the scholar in the use of critical and historical methods.[37] Even though the use of traditional phrases obscures this point, the constitution's basic position is that the Bible is a thoroughly human book which does not derive its authority from special inter-

---

[36] Skydsgaard, "Scripture and Tradition," *op. cit.* (n. 13, p. 102 above), pp. 34–40.
[37] *Ibid.*, pp. 40–44.

ventions of the Holy Spirit exempting its authors from the erroneous opinions prevalent in their milieu. The Bible's authority arises, rather, from the fact that these authors, writing under a guidance which is nonetheless divine for being primarily "providential"[38] rather than "miraculous," are our primary witnesses to God's saving revelation of himself.

This acceptance of modern historical-critical methods of studying the Bible is of fundamental ecumenical importance. As has often been remarked, the exegetes who use these methods can no longer be divided along confessional lines. Catholics and Protestants find themselves agreeing on what the biblical authors intended even in regard to the most hotly debated issues of the past.

It is true that more than this is needed for doctrinal *rapprochement*. There must be the recognition that not only Scripture but also the doctrinal traditions of the various churches are historically conditioned. This involves openness to theological diversity, to the need for constantly reinterpreting the faith in the light of new and different situations and modes of thought. By itself, however, this simply leads to chaos, and so another and final condition must be added. There must be a genuine acknowledgment of the normative status for Christian faith of the scriptural witness to God's revelation; there must be a devout and unabashed attachment to the full range of biblical claims, however incredible they may seem to either ancient or modern man.

Among the Catholic and Protestant theologians who to some substantial degree meet these conditions, an astonishing convergence has already occurred. Rahner and Barth, Pannenberg and Metz, and even Küng and Käsemann are in basic agreement on point after controverted point. These men, as well as many others who could be cited, represent a great variety of theological interpretations, but they are genuinely united on the dogmatic level by their adherence to a common revelational center. They proceed, one might say, not by accommodating revelation to the new, but conversely, by interpreting the new worlds of thought and action

---

[38] For the "providential" view of inspiration, see K. Rahner, "Inspiration in the Bible," *Inquiries* (New York: Herder & Herder, 1964), pp. 7–86.

in terms of revelation. Thus they are quite unlike the Gnostics, Latin Averroists, many Renaissance humanists, nineteenth-century liberals, and twentieth-century radical theologians who attenuate or mutilate the basic Christian affirmations in order to make them believable in terms of some contemporary procrustean framework of thought. Instead they stand in the line of the Greek and Latin Fathers, Augustine, Aquinas, Luther, Calvin, and their successors, who reshape whatever convictions they may have about the world, whether Platonic, Aristotelian, late medieval, or modern evolutionary in the light of their primary commitment to the reality and truth which is in Jesus Christ. They strive to "compel every human thought to surrender in obedience to Christ" (II Cor. 10:5 [NEB]), and in so doing find themselves drawing closer together, not in an impoverishing uniformity, but in an enriching diversity of perspectives within what is recognizably the same faith.

The higher evaluation and new understanding of the role of Scripture which have made this development possible on the Roman Catholic side are not, as we have seen, fully or consistently articulated by Vatican II. Much of its phrasing is reminiscent of traditionalist views of the Bible, tradition, and infallible dogmatic authority. Nevertheless, there is enough of the new in the Council's documents to give solid support to a Catholic form of the *sola scriptura.* And if our thesis throughout this book is correct, that it is the new which is likely to be decisive, then we must say that the dogmatic barriers to greater faithfulness to the Bible have now been breached.

Yet the Protestant, however much he will welcome these changes, cannot be fully satisfied. The more stringent Reformation understanding of the normative role of Scripture still remains mandatory. There is reason now as in the past to consider it an essential help in preserving the lordship of Christ over theology and the church. It makes unmistakably clear that the public revelation which culminates and is summed up in Christ is closed, is final, until the day of his return. It is true that the tradition must develop, that new dogmas marking the limits between orthodoxy and heterodoxy are necessary for the sake of the faithfulness of the church's witness to the gospel. This was necessary against the Arians in the fourth century and against medieval semi-Pelagianism in the sixteenth. It was also necessary against the Deutsche Christen at Barmen in 1934. It is necessary now against racial segregation in the church, simply to cite one vital issue of our own day. But what we must insist is that no dogmatic decision of the church can go beyond what faithfulness to Christ (as witnessed to in Scripture) clearly demands; this applies to any situation even where the church is compelled to take a stand on a problem which has become of vital importance to the authenticity of its Christian witness. It cannot, as the Roman Catholic Church has done in its papal and Marian dogmas, go beyond what faithfulness to Scripture clearly requires.

It is of some importance to note, even at the cost of repetition, the point of this criticism. It may be granted, at least for the sake of dialogue with Roman Catholic theologians, that the papal and Marian dogmas can be interpreted in theology and perhaps even in practice (though that day may still be far removed) in such a sense that they are harmonizable with Scripture, that they are, so to speak, acceptable theological or pious opinions. But no competent Roman Catholic seriously maintains that there are not other exegetically possible ways of understanding the role of the pope and of Mary in God's plans. And because these doctrines are not the only available alternatives consonant with Scripture on objective exegetical grounds, they cannot be made dogmas, they cannot be made *de fide*. To do so is to run the danger, in practice, even if not in theory, of adding to the supremely authoritative public revelation which centers in Christ and is testified to in the Bible.

Further, no dogmas, not even the ones which express legitimate and necessary decisions and of whose correctness the church is thoroughly and rightfully assured, can be formally declared "infallible" and "irreformable" or "irreversible." To declare them infallible, even in the restricted sense which we have reviewed, is to assert that the church is empowered to exempt some of its teachings from God's eschatological judgment. It is to deny that there is an element of risk in faith and thus also in every effort to formulate the faith. For these reasons those who are the heirs of the Reformation must continue to insist that the *sola scriptura* and the lordship of Christ to which it testifies forbid the supposition that there are any institutionalized teaching offices in the church, whether pope, council, or theological faculty, which are absolutely guaranteed even a minimal degree of indefectibility or infallibility.

These affirmations, however, must be made without self-righteousness in full recognition that those who are not as clear doctrinally on this and other points as Protestants believe themselves to be may nevertheless concretely in many ways be more faithful than Protestants to Christ and the scriptural witness to him. In the light of present trends, it would not be at all surprising if the Church of Rome becomes the church of the Bible to a greater extent than are many of the bodies which pride themselves on their Reformation heritage. This is a sobering thought, and it is perhaps the chief lesson to be learned by Protestants from a consideration of this part of the accomplishments of Vatican II.

In concluding this book there is no need to review its argument in detail. I have attempted to sketch what seem to me the genuinely new elements in the teaching of the Second Vatican Council: its realistically eschatological vision of the world, of the church as the pilgrim people of God, of *diakonia, leitourgia,* and *koinonia,* and of the relation of Scripture to revelation, tradition, dogma, and the magisterium. The developments which have taken place in each of these areas do not constitute a systematic unity. The Constitutions on the Liturgy and on Revelation, for example, show no trace of a specifically realistic eschatological outlook and little awareness of the pilgrim character of the church. Yet all the major documents have clearly abandoned the classical framework of thought with its triumphalist and authoritarian view of the church, individualistic notion of worship and religious experience, and intellectualistic concept of revelation. They all recognize the importance of history and diversity, and insist that the church's central task in a pluralistic world is to serve, embody, and manifest God's universally reconciling act in Christ. To a remarkable degree, therefore, the new elements cohere with one another. They display a unity which, while not that of a theological system, constitutes a sphere of theological discourse and conceptualization which is sharply and definably different from that which has prevailed in Roman Catholic magisterial teaching ever since the Middle Ages.

The new, we have noted, is mixed with the old, but it is the new which is likely to shape the future. To the extent that this happens, we shall be confronted by a Catholicism which, while in one sense adhering to its dogmas and traditions, now interprets them afresh. It will not be a variant of either old or new forms of Protestantism, but it will nevertheless be exempt from almost all the Reformation doctrinal criticisms. The only historic issue which I personally still see no possibility of resolving without loss of self-identity on either side is that of magisterial infallibility in general or papal infallibility in particular; but even that could conceivably be so reduced in importance that staunch Catholics and staunch Protestants, each genuinely heirs of their respective traditions, would be forced to ask seriously whether their remaining differences justify continued separation.

This is not necessarily a possibility so distant that serious consideration of it can be indefinitely postponed. Undoubtedly vast changes must take place in the concrete life of Protestant and Catholic churches before large-scale reunion becomes practicable. But theologians are obligated to think in terms of the truth of the gospel, and where no crucial disagreements remain on this, they are duty bound to denounce continuing disunity as sinful, as against God's will. There is evidence that many of the most devoted Christians and best theological minds in the younger generation of both Catholics and Protestants are already finding themselves driven to take this stand. They know themselves to be one in Christ, they are sufficiently well-informed and intellectually honest to see that the doctrinal barriers are not insurmountable, and consequently they find the institutional inertia of their churches intolerable in view of the need for united service and witness to the Lord who has come and is coming again.

Our final word, therefore, must be that the theological issues raised by Vatican II are no less urgent for Protestants than for Catholics. This Council has opened up immense possibilities for the growing together of the Christian family, but whether they are actualized, and how they are actualized, depends on the collaboration of all the confessions.

INDEX

INDEX

Type, 11 on 13 and 10 on 11 Garamond
Display, Columna and Garamond